It's All about Your Bottom Line
Developing Accounts Payable
Issues and Practices

Mary S. Schaeffer

Mary S. Schaeffer

Table of Contents

Left blank on purpose

Preface

Without a doubt, the business world is changing and along with it the accounts payable function. These changes, if not recognized and dealt with appropriately can have a huge negative impact on any organization's bottom line. In order to remain competitive, no organization can afford excess expenses or losses due to poor practices. Technology has definitely played its part, but there are other not-so-readily recognizable factors that come into play.

I spend my days immersed in accounts payable issues, talking to experts as well as practitioners handling the day-to-day details of the function, reading the latest reports from bankers, fraud experts, regulatory authorities and others involved in the payment arena. This provides me with the unique perspective and the insights needed to identify emerging issues and pinpoint the new practices needed to deal with them.

The basic accounts payable function has not changed; it is still about getting the organization's bills paid. But the breadth of knowledge and expertise needed to address the challenges every company faces today has expanded exponentially. Using yesterday's best practices to address tomorrow's problems just won't cut it. The impact will be felt in your bottom line. That's why I wrote this book; not to explain the intricacies of running an efficient and effective accounts payable function but how to

1

deal with the newest challenges presented by today's developing issues.

The book begins with a look at changing best practices and identifies those which must change in order for the accounts payable function to remain effective and thus allow the parent organization to remain competitive. It also explains why best practices are so important and why keeping current on the latest practices is critical for all.

The next issue investigated is the seemingly simple one of invoices. But it is anything but uncomplicated. On the face of it, it would seem that technology should have made invoice processing easier. And, in many cases it has. However, there has been an unexpected complication and virtually every organization now finds itself handling an excess of duplicate invoices, which are not always readily identifiable. As one manager said in disgust, "we now have more invoices than ever before and it's not because our business has expanded."

After addressing the invoice issue, it's time to look at payment concerns. In a long-overdue move, a good number of companies have finally started making electronic (ACH) payments in the US. Such a move does not come without challenges and unexpected hiccups and they are addressed. Once a company has an electronic payment program up and running, most want to expand their program. And that does not come without some precise efforts on the part of the paying organization. There have been and we are expecting more innovation in the payment area and as such have devoted two chapters to the problems surrounding it.

Payments to vendors aren't the only type of payments companies make. They also have to reimburse their employees for business travel and entertainment expenses. What's gone on in this arena is amazing. Just as companies are finding that technology enables the influx of numerous copies of invoices, some companies have discovered it also enable their employees to submit the same expense multiple times. Whether this is an honest mistake or a deliberate attempt to defraud the company is not always clear. What is apparent is that companies have to recognize the problem and address it. We take on the whole receipt issue exploring some of the developing practices now needed.

Expense reimbursement fraud is just the tip of the iceberg when it comes to the theft issue. There have been explosions of new frauds, many of which are directed squarely at the personnel working in accounts payable. One of the latest is aimed at executives in the C-level suite. All are devious and require an understanding of the frauds and the installation of new processes and procedures to ensure your organization doesn't get hit.

Turning our attention away from expense reports, the next issue to be addressed is a brand new one. You may think you know what a vendor portal is but the chances are high that your definition will be somewhat different than that of the person sitting next to you. And, that is one of the many challenges when dealing with some of the newest technology to hit the accounts payable function in some time. Different service providers are using the term, vendor portal, to describe different services. We'll discuss the various iterations of this term and then take a look at where this technology is going.

Besides the portals, there's a lot of technology in accounts payable today. In fact, there is so much to discuss when it comes to technology and accounts payable that we've divided the material into two chapters. The first addresses the issues related directly to the function and the second to the myriad of new concerns related to personal devices, primarily smartphones and tablets. No organization can afford to ignore the impact they are having on processes and internal controls.

And of course, no book on accounts payable issues would be complete without addressing the massive issue of internal controls. In particular, we take a look at what we call control breakdowns, for those are the issues that make a fraud easier to perpetrate. Some of the areas identified just may surprise you.

With all the change and the new technology, you are probably aware of a ton of new vocabulary. Words that a year or two ago would have been completely foreign now roll off our tongue as though they had been with us forever. In the chapter on vocabulary we provide a roundup of new terminology. Now some of you may recognize some of it, but we're almost certain that everyone will find a new term or two or twenty they weren't conversant with.

As we come to the end of the book, we have two roundup chapters. The first focuses on the function itself, looking into a crystal ball predicting what the accounts payable function will look like down the road. And, the second provides insights for the professionals who want to work in the field. It provides guidance as to what type of skills they should make sure they have. The controllers, CFOs and other managers reading this may also get an insight or two from it.

Clearly, these issues are important to those organizations that want to run a cost-effective, efficient, fraud-resistant accounts payable function. And for a very good reason, after all, It's All about Your Bottom Line!

Chapter 1

Changing Best Practices:
No Longer a Static Set of Rules

There has been relentless pressure to improve the bottom line for years. That certainly isn't news. But what is different is the amount of attention the accounts payable function is receiving in that regards. Whether it's viewed as the last bastion where savings can be found or it has finally gotten the attention it has long deserved isn't relevant. What is important is that companies focus on those issues that can make a difference, for there are quite a few opportunities in the accounts payable process.

Complicating the matter is the fact that the accounts payable function has been undergoing some seismic changes in the last few years. Technology, new frauds, and an explosion of regulatory issues (both new ones and the greater enforcement of legislation already on the books) have caused the accounts payable function to come under greater scrutiny. All this has come together to offer a great opportunity – for organizations to either take advantage of the change and improve the bottom line or fall on their faces by not recognizing the opportunity.

That's why, best practices are more important than ever. Unfortunately, the definition of what is a best practice when it comes to various accounts payable functions has been changing. What's more, areas that formally were of little import are now more important than ever – although, until you examine the issue, it is often not readily apparent.

In this chapter we'll examine:

- Why Best Practices in Accounts Payable Matter
- Changing Best Practices in Accounts Payable for an Efficient and Cost-Effective Function
- Changing Best Practices in Accounts Payable to Fight Fraud and Tighten Controls

Why Best Practices in Accounts Payable Really Do Matter

From time to time, a senior level executive will demand to know "what's the big deal about accounts payable?" These folks think that an effective accounts payable process is one where someone sits at a desk and simply writes checks for any invoice that crosses their desk. While this view is not as prevalent as it once was, it still exists. For that reason we think it a good idea to investigate what can go wrong when accounts payable best practices are not used. Here's a look at what could go wrong should an organization be foolish enough to follow such a practice.

Reason #10: The organization would end up paying many invoices twice. This is because some vendors send invoices twice as a matter of practice (e-mail and postal mail) while others only send that second invoice when a payment is late. Whatever the reason for the sending of the second invoice, an organization not employing best practices and strong internal controls would result in duplicate payments – which vendors rarely return unless asked.

Reason #9: The organization would be hit with more fraud. Once crooks realized that the organization was paying whatever invoices came its way, the less than honest ones would start sending double and triple invoices and perhaps even some for goods and services not purchased.

Reason #8: As long as the organization was not concerned about the bottom line (and virtually all are!) ignoring best practices would be fine. For duplicate invoices and other excess expenses come right off the bottom line impacting the profitability of the organization in a negative manner.

Reason #7: When best practices are not followed, payments are typically delayed. This does not sit well with vendors. Typically, when payments are delayed, vendors have a difficult time getting a straight answer as to when they can expect their payments. None of this is conducive to strong relations and hence vendor relations tend to be damaged.

Reason #6: While best practices result in an efficient accounts payable function, the reverse is true when best practices are ignored. The end result is that additional staff will be needed to handle the same amount of work.

Reason #5: It will come as no surprise to those reading this to learn that inefficient processes lead to increased expense for the accounts payable function. This may come in the form of extra staff, lost early payment discounts or late fees.

Reason #4: While most would like to forget about the Sarbanes-Oxley Act, those in the public arena don't have that luxury. Since best practices go hand-in-hand with strong internal controls, no public company can afford to ignore the issue of best practices. It should also be noted that some private companies are subject to the strictures of Sarbanes-Oxley either because their lenders demand it or a large customer will only do business with organizations that are S-Ox compliant.

Reason #3: Often times, not employing best practices results in inaccurate information which trickles down to the financial statements resulting in inaccurate financial statements. This is a worst case scenario and one that every organization should strive to avoid. It can also mean being singled out by auditors (internal or external) for financial statement issues. This is not an area where most accounts payable departments have any interest in being mentioned and most strive to avoid it.

Reason #2: Inaccurate financial statements and financial reporting can lead to trouble for executives relying on faulty financial information for business decisions. Use of best practices in the accounts payable arena can lead to improved forecasting, especially when it comes to cash flow.

Reason #1: If everything discussed so far has not been enough to convince you that best practices are a necessity, consider the following. By not using best practices across the entire accounts payable function you could be courting trouble with the IRS and state taxing authorities. All are looking for funds to bolster their sagging coffers. For example, many believe that under reporting of income by independent contractors and other self-employed individuals is largely responsible for the tax gap. The attention on this issue is focused on the corporate world for sometimes questionable practices when it comes to 1099 reporting.

Along the same lines, many believe that only one-third of all organizations that should be reporting and remitting unclaimed property are actually doing so. The result is that many organizations are wide open for trouble in this regards. And, you don't have to go far to find a story bewailing online sales on the Internet and its impact on the states collection of sales and use tax.

Given these issues and others, it is imperative that all organizations look at their accounts payable function and employ as many best practices as they can integrate across the entire cycle.

Changing Best Practices in AP for an Efficient and Cost-Effective Function

Some of the new best practices in use in accounts payable today are not necessarily a result of some spiffy new technology or in reaction to a new fraud but rather are just a modification in the way the process is handled due to the evolving business environment. Let's make no mistake about it; affordable technology, increased regulatory pressures and new frauds have played a role. But, the new practices in use by a growing number of leading-edge organizations are a reflection of this transformed environment.

The new practices discussed in this section are the ones that make for a more efficient and cost effective process. The next section will focus on changes now in use to instill tighter controls and fight fraud. They all involve process changes rather than an expenditure for software or hardware. You may already have integrated some or all of these practices into your operation.

Practice #1: There is a greater emphasis on analytics as a means to improve the process and tighten controls. As the process gains more visibility within the organization, there is a growing recognition that the accounts payable data contains a gold mine of information. Whether the organization just uses Excel to the max or relies on the new and emerging big data products, there's a lot of business intelligence stored away in that data.

Practice #2: Get a Form W-9 from every new vendor. This is something that has been recommended for the last few years and it is starting to get traction. At a recent accounts receivable event, over half the participants indicated their customers were requiring a W-9 before making payment. So, you should get less pushback from your suppliers when you ask for this. In fact, many will have an electronic one ready to email you, if you ask.

Practice #3: Insist on ACH (electronic payment) for all rush payments. This works particularly well in those organizations where there is a serious move to convert as many vendors to electronic payments as possible. It also averts problems with positive pay when the rush item can't be included in the positive pay file for a day or two.

Practice #4: Issue ACH payments more frequently than check payments. This is a subtle but sneaky trick to "encourage" vendors to accept electronic payments. Organizations that have had the most success with this approach are those who gradually decrease the number of check runs in comparison to the frequency of their electronic payments. So, they may start out with one check run and two ACH runs a week and gradually move to two check runs a month and then perhaps one.

Practice #5: Return invoices that do not show a PO number or name of a requisitioner. When looking to eliminate tasks that add no value, the handling of invoices without identifying information is right at the top of the list. It wastes not only the time of the person trying to figure out who should approve the invoice but also that of everyone interrupted in the process. There is no reason why anyone should submit an invoice without either a PO number or the name of the requisitioner. Create a polite form letter indicating your organization's requirements that this information be included on all invoices. Then attach it to any invoice missing this information and send it back to the vendor. If you phrase your request in terms of what is needed in order to get the invoice paid in a more timely manner, the vendor should not be offended.

Practice #6: Set up a separate e-mail address to accept invoices submitted by e-mail. Fewer and fewer suppliers are willing to print and mail invoices; it's just too expensive. Those not using invoice automation are e-mailing invoices. To keep control of this workflow, set up a separate e-mail account for invoices and direct vendors to send invoices to it. If they continue to send invoices to private e-mail accounts, some will not be forwarded to accounts payable in a timely manner.

Practice #7: Set up a separate fax machine/number to accept faxed invoices. Some vendors offer their customers the option of having invoices faxed instead of e-mailed. This approach works particularly well when the fax number is tied to an e-mail and the fax is converted. These e-fax facilities are not expensive at all.

Practice #8: Make the cleansing of the master vendor file an ongoing process rather than an annual or bi-annual project. As the recognition of the importance of the master vendor file can play in a slew of issues grows so does the realization that cleansing the master vendor file once every year or two or more doesn't work. There is a move toward more frequent cleansing making it part of the regular process.

Practice #9: Conduct regular statement audits for all vendors. This is a relatively easy way to identify funds sitting with vendors that belong to your organization. These are funds that add to your bottom line. Unfortunately, for a variety of reasons, this money often goes undetected by the rightful owners and eventually it disappears. It is your money and your responsibility for finding and recovering it.

Practice #10: With the explosion of personal devices (smartphones, tablets etc.) in the hands of individual employees, it was inevitable that some conscientious employees would find ways to use these devices to become more efficient at work. This can create problems as most of these devices do not have the same fraud and anti-virus protections as desktop computers. Nor are these protections updated on a regular basis. They can have the same protections – if the issue is addressed and protocols established. Thus, a growing number of organizations are addressing the issue, commonly referred to as BYOD (bring your own device). It is imperative that every organization establish such a policy.

How many of these process changes have you introduced into your organization's accounts payable function?

Changing Best Practices in AP to Fight Fraud and Tighten Controls

This section focuses on those changing best practices that will help in the fraud arena. The new practices discussed in this piece are the ones that focus on changes now in use to instill tighter controls and fight fraud. As with the practices discussed above, they all involve process changes rather than an expenditure for software or hardware. You may already have integrated some or all of these practices into your operation. Crooks understand banking and technology far better than the average business person. And, they are using this knowledge to find ways to get their hands on your organization's money. Don't let them. Take the appropriate steps to make sure they are not successful. That will include:

Practice #1: Keeping up now means keeping up with new frauds and new fraud prevention techniques. Unfortunately, it's not only businesses taking advantage of new technology to improve their processes, crooks are as well. What is truly regrettable is the understanding these fraudsters have of the banking system and the ingenuity they have used to devise new frauds. This is an ongoing requirement, not something you can do once and then forget about it.

Practice #2: Job rotation is not something we normally thought about in accounts payable. But, if you have more than two or three processors, consider moving them around rather than leaving them handling the same vendors for years on end. Yes, the benefit of that approach is they get to know the account really well. This can be beneficial in resolving problems or if you have to ask for a special favor. However, and this is a biggie, it also means they may get so friendly, a few will concoct a plan to defraud one or both organizations. While this won't happen often, it has occurred frequently enough for fraud experts to recommend this course of action.

Practice #3: Likewise, mandatory vacations help protect an organization against an ongoing employee fraud. The theory beyond this recommendation is that if an employee is perpetrating an ongoing fraud, it will unravel if they are forced to be away from the office for five (or more) consecutive days. For this tactic to be effective, it is imperative that someone other than the employee perform their job during this period. The strategy falls apart if the employee simply performs his or her job from home.

Practice #4: Rather than have employees handling online

banking use their own computers for this task, designate a single PC for online banking activities. This computer should be used for NOTHING else, especially e-mail or surfing the Internet. This tactic protects the organization against a corporate account takeover by savvy fraudsters who utilize the Internet to perpetrate their crimes. While this does not happen often, the damage it inflicts when it does occur is massive and every organization, regardless of size, is advised to protect against it. The cost of a computer is small so there is no financial reason for ignoring this piece of advice.

Practice #5: When responding to an e-mail, especially if it has anything to do with finances (like changes to bank account information), hit the forward key instead of the reply key to respond to confirm. When you hit the forward key, you will have to type in the e-mail address of the person you are responding to. If it is someone you regularly do business with, the address should auto-fill. When the message is sent, if the party you thought had sent the original note did not, he or she will respond accordingly – and you will not have honored a request from a crook. Spoofing of e-mail addresses is just one more way fraudsters attempt to get their hands on your organization's funds.

Practice #6: Close off system access for employees who have either been promoted or who have left the company. This step is often overlooked and leaves the organization wide open to segregation of duties issues. By closing off the access as part of the organization's standard separation and promotion practices, this threat is eliminated. Some groups neglect to do this for departing employees forgetting that a few of them may be hired back at a future date.

Practice #7: Check the OFAC list at least monthly to ensure payments are not going to parties on the SDN list. The reality is you are supposed to check payments against this list before you make each payment, but few other than the credit card companies actually do this. Some make it a part of the new vendor set-up to check against the list. This is a good first step.

If you simply can't incorporate the practice of checking before each payment, try and do it at least once a month. At least this will demonstrate a good-faith effort on your part to conform with the law. In Canada, check against the OSFI list.

Practice #8: Provide some FCPA training for the accounts payable staff. As several recent high-profile cases demonstrate, the Department of Justice is serious about enforcing the anti-bribery legislation currently on the books. By providing the accounts payable staff, the last set of eyes to see a payment before it goes out the door, with some training on what to look for, the organization can show good faith, if it inadvertently makes a bribe.

Practice #9: Regularly update contact information in the master vendor file in order to help protect the organization against fraud. This way, when a questionable transaction shows up, you can contact the legitimate vendor to get clarification. If you haven't ever collected contact information or haven't updated it, this task will become infinitely more difficult. There's more at the end of this chapter on this issue.

Practice #10: A growing number of organizations are now requiring the detailed meal receipt for restaurant expenditures. The reason for this is simple. Too many employees play games with their expense reimbursement requests and companies have had enough. What's more, the detailed meal receipt helps those with grants that include special requirements related to reimbursable meals.

Chapter 2

The Evolution in the Invoice Environment

Invoices remain the mainstay of the accounts payable function and the primary way companies get paid. That being said, today's invoices and the way they are handled are very different than in the past. With the move to automation of invoice processing, an emphasis on cost reduction (including the costs associated with printing and mailing invoices) and a greater reliance on e-mail, every organization needs to reexamine their invoice processes, especially their receipt process. In this chapter we examine:

- The Shifting Invoice Landscape and the Emerging Practices Needed to Stay Current
- A Best Practice Check List for Receipt of Invoices
- Why PDF Invoice Copies Make A Lot of Sense
- An Efficient Process for Handling Invoices Sent by e-Mail
- A Policy for Vendors Submitting Invoices for Payment by e-Mail Only
- How to Stop Vendors from Sending Duplicate Invoices
- A Game Plan to Weed out Duplicate Invoices

The Shifting Invoice Landscape and the Emerging Practices Needed to Stay Current

This means it is critical that every organization regularly review their invoice handling procedures to ensure they are still adequate and provide the strong internal controls needed to address today's evolving issues. Let's take a look at some of the changes along with some action steps to address them. We'll start with the easiest.

Change #1: While organizations continue to send duplicate invoices, they never/rarely mark them as such. It is up to the company receiving them to weed out the duplicates.

This is important because, as readers are painfully aware, few vendors return those second payments unless prompted to do so, after research by the payor or its agent. Both use valuable resources better spent elsewhere.

Action: Beef up your routines to identify duplicate invoices. It is now more important than ever that the vendor's invoice number be entered accurately.

Change #2: Invoices are being emailed in ever increasing numbers. They are a reality of today's workplace. Refusing to accept emailed invoices is not a workable solution.

Action: Create a policy to handle e-mailed invoices. This should address where they should be sent (ideally one centralized e-mail address that is not associated with an individual) and how they should be stored and processed.

If the company is using an automated invoice processing approach, allowances must be made for e-mailed invoices.

Change #3: Invoices increasingly are likely to be sent more than once. This might be because the invoice is mailed and emailed; because payment was late and it was sent a second time or it is emailed to several people within the organization. The cause is less important than the issue of the increasing workload.

Action: This increased workload demands that the duplicate be identified early in the process rather than at the last minute, right before the payment goes out the door. Begin by identifying vendors who are sending invoices either using duplicate mediums or to duplicate recipients and ask them to stop.

Change #4: Invoices are now being sent through a variety of channels. Today, accounts payable departments might be asked by suppliers to accept emailed invoices, faxed invoices, EDI transmissions, as well as invoices delivered by a variety of e-invoicing third parties services. This is all in addition to paper invoices delivered by the post. While eventually this will all shake out, for the time being, invoices are coming at us from multiple sources.

Action: Adjust your processes to accommodate all methods of invoice delivery. Make sure you incorporate routines to identify those being sent a second time.

Change #5: Invoices are being sent through a variety of different electronic protocols. There are over 30 service providers providing electronic invoicing services to the vendor community. In theory, you could receive invoices from all of them.

This is in addition to the proprietary invoice delivery protocols developed by some very large companies. A few of these require the customers to "pick up" their invoices. And at this point, there is no standard architecture. Some of the more advanced services have the ability to incorporate invoices sent from other providers, but not all have that ability — yet.

Action: This is just another facet of the flexibility needed in accounts payable when it comes to invoice handling. Each time you are presented with a new protocol, develop a process for it so the outcome matches that of the rest of your processing. Eventually, this issue may go away, but for the next few years it is something every organization will have to adapt to.

Change #6: Fraudulent invoice activity is up. This is really not surprising given the ease and low cost of emailing invoices. While some of the phony invoices are clearly fraudulent, some are not as obvious as the crooks involved understand what they are doing and how to effectively manipulate the marketplace.

Action: The same controls that help weed out duplicate invoices should help identify fraudulent invoices. Strong internal controls, stringent coding standards and good invoice handling practices will go a long way towards making sure your organization doesn't end up paying an invoice that is fraudulent.

Change #7: In certain parts of the world there has been a move towards mandatory electronic invoicing. The motivating factor behind this stance is the desire on the part of the governments involved to ensure they receive all the tax revenues they are owed.

If electronic invoicing is used, and it is sent through a government sponsored facility, there is a greater chance taxes will be paid on that revenue. It has been a huge success in the countries that are using it. Virtually all report an increase in tax revenues.

Action: While mandatory electronic invoicing is not in place in either the US or Canada, we watch with great interest the development of this approach in other parts of the world. One can safely assume that if the initial success continues, those countries not adopting a mandatory electronic invoicing stance will look at the process with great interest.

Therefore, it is advisable that every organization begin to investigate electronic invoicing and develop capabilities to accept electronic invoices, if they have not already begun to do so. There are many benefits associated with a paperless approach to invoice receipt and processing aside from the regulatory issue.

Concluding Thoughts

Electronic invoicing has been around for two decades or more. The dream of a paperless office and the discussion of it have been going on for at least half that time.

Finally, it looks like that dream of an office uncluttered by paper may be finally close to becoming a reality. Invoice handling has changed a lot in the last decade and it probably will continue to evolve in the next few years.

Have you incorporated all the changes discussed above in your department's practices? Are you prepared for the future of invoice handling?

A Best Practice Check List for Receipt of Invoices

Perhaps one of the biggest changes in accounts payable has now come to that most mundane of functions—the receipt of the invoice. No longer is this simply a mail function with the professionals focused on educating the mail room personnel—no, technology and the high cost of postage have turned this basic function on its head. In response AP Now has compiled this checklist for how all organizations should receive their invoices.

1. Have all invoices mailed to one location, ideally accounts payable. This gets the invoices logged in, limits the who's-got-the-invoice games, puts you in the best position to earn as many early payment discounts as possible and, in general, leads to a more efficient invoice handling process.

2. Contact any vendor not mailing invoices to the correct location and provide the correct mail-to address.

3. Set up a dedicated fax line to receive faxed invoices. It should be in a relatively secure location in the accounts payable department and used for nothing but the receipt of invoices. No one other than those designated in your policies and procedures should be permitted to take documents from that machine.

4. Set up a separate e-mail account for the receipt of invoices. It should only be used for the receipt of invoices and not for personal e-mail. The address should be something like invoices@abccompany.com not a personal e-mail address. Someone should be assigned to check the accounts several times a day. When the person assigned that task is out of the

office, the responsibility should go to someone else just as opening the mail would be.

5. Write up instructions for your welcome packet that includes directions on how to mail, fax, or e-mail invoices. This information should also be distributed to current vendors.

6. Forget the "Only pay from an original invoice" control. It doesn't work. With today's technology there can be numerous "original invoices."

7. Encourage faxed and e-mailed invoices. Since they appear to be a fact of life, you may as well get the most out of them. By receiving them earlier in the process, you will have more time to handle the invoices, resolve discrepancies, and hopefully earn all the early payment discounts to which you are entitled.

An Efficient Process for Handling Invoices Sent by e-Mail

Trying to stop vendors from sending invoices by e-mail is like trying to stop the water once the dam or levy has broken. Given the inevitability of e-mailed invoices, it is far better to develop an effective plan to take advantage of this new delivery method than to fight it. What follows is a rather simple seven-step process any organization can use to address the receipt of e-mailed invoices situation.

- **Step 1**: Recognize that you can't fight the proverbial City Hall and establish a formal policy for handling e-mailed invoices. This should be part of your formal policy and procedures manual for the accounts payable function.

- **Step 2**: Set up one e-mail address to receive invoices from suppliers. This should be part of your best practice strategy to receive all e-mails in one centralized location. Today that means one postal address, one e-mail address and one fax address. The e-mail address should not be a personal address but one that can be accessed by several people. This way, if someone is unexpectedly out of the office or leaves the company, there is no disruption to vendors e-mailing invoices.

- **Step 3**: Provide the email address established for the receipt of invoices to all suppliers. This can be done in both the Welcome Packet for new vendors and the annual letter to vendors. If you normally don't send an annual letter to vendors, you might send a special communication regarding this e-mail address.

- **Step 4**: Vendors should be informed that only invoices should be sent to this address. Nothing else sent to that address will be forwarded to other parties.

- **Step 5**: Vendors should be instructed not to send a second invoice by snail mail. Be aware that some will disregard this directive. Watch this process and create a list of vendors who always double submit despite your instructions. Paper invoices from these vendors should be discarded.

- **Step 6**: Different people should be assigned to monitor the account on different days. They can also fill in for each other when someone is out or on vacations.

- **Step 7**: Upon receipt of an invoice, it should immediately be reviewed and forwarded to the appropriate party for approval.

Typically, e-mailed invoices are first turned into a PDF and then sent to the customer. Great care needs to be taken that each is only processed once. For if you print the PDF, the hundredth printing will look just as good as the first one and you won't be able to tell which is the original and which is the copy. This means that routines for weeding out duplicates are more important than ever. It should also entail duplicate payment checking routines be integrated into the invoice processing function.

Invoices that are e-mailed are a reality every organization has to deal with. Trying to avoid the issue is not smart. Following a game plan, such as the one discussed above, is your best strategy for making this new approach work for your organization.

Making the Most of No-Cost Technology: A Policy for Vendors Submitting Invoices for Payment by e-Mail Only

No longer does an organization have to spend a small fortune to gain the benefits of technology and/or to go paperless. In fact, AP Now has found a number of organizations who are using no-cost technology to streamline their accounts payable operations, in unique ways. What follows is an amalgamation of the process used in several organizations to receive e-mail.

The Basic Philosophy

The organizations who take this approach have decided they are fed up with all the paper and want to eliminate as much of it as possible. Yet, they are not ready to sign up for an automated invoice processing service offered by third-party providers.

They have decided to encourage suppliers to send invoices via e-mail. Many of the companies that go down this road are already receiving some (most) of their invoices in this manner. Suppliers are asked to convert their invoices to a PDF and then e-mail them in.

Some offer a fax alternative for those vendors who don't seem to be able to create a PDF of their invoices. Of course, what these suppliers don't realize is that the company has married its fax with an e-fax service, so they are not receiving the paper, but an e-mail of the fax.

The Invoice by E-mail Only Policy

By getting all invoices electronically, paper invoices no longer are a factor. Here's several sample policies you can use:

1) All vendors are encouraged to submit their invoices by e-mail.

2) All vendors are required to submit their invoices by e-mail.

3) All vendors are required to submit their invoices by e-mail or fax.

Which approach you decide to take, will depend on your philosophy and your tolerance for the headache dealing with paper invoices.

When receiving invoices by e-mail, a separate address should be set up for this purpose. Do not use an employee's e-mail for this purpose. It creates too many problems when the employee is out unexpectedly or on vacation. It also increases the chance of getting lost. Also, several people should have access to this e-mail account, so there is adequate backup when the primary employee is absent. Some organizations divide the responsibility for checking the invoice e-mail account between several employees.

Best Practices for E-mailed Invoices

Suppliers should be provided with some guidelines for submitting invoices by e-mail. Here are a few best practices regarding that issue:

- **Best Practice #1:** The subject line should include a standard statement such as Invoice Attached and the PO number.

- **Best Practice # 2:** Invoices should be sent to the e-mail address and nowhere else. There is no need to send copies to other parties. This just increases the chances of them being processed and possibly paid twice.

- **Best Practice # 3:** Each invoice should be in a separate PDF.

- **Best Practice # 4:** If there is backup documentation, that may be included in the same PDF file, although the invoice must be the first page.

- **Best Practice # 5:** Each invoice should be sent in a separate e-mail.

- **Best Practice # 6:** There is no need to include a cover memo or note with the invoice. The first page of the PDF file should be the invoice itself.

- **Best Practice # 7:** The PDF should be sent as an attachment. Invoice information should not be pasted into the body of the e-mail message.

- **Best Practice # 8:** Statements and other correspondence should not be sent to the e-mail address set up for the receipt of invoices.

Other Invoice Policies

Regardless of the approach taken, there are some basics that should be incorporated into the invoice receipt policy. These should be shared with vendors. They include:

1) All invoices must include a PO number or the name of the purchaser

2) All invoices should be centrally received and the e-mail address and/or fax number and/or postal address provided to the vendor

Would accepting invoices only by e-mail make your accounts payable operation run a little bit smoother? If so, you might want to investigate adopting such a policy.

8 Reasons Why PDF Invoice Copies Make A Lot of Sense

While it would be nice to receive all invoices electronically through one of the third party systems that automates the three-way match and schedules items for payment, that is not the world most accounts payable professionals live in. Most still end up with a large, albeit diminishing, number of paper invoices.

Within the last few years, a growing number of companies of all sizes have begun emailing pdf copies of their invoices. It's cheaper for them and the invoice gets into the hands of the intended recipient faster. What's more, the quicker an invoice arrives at the customers' accounts payable department, the faster it is likely to be paid. Still, for some time, a number of accounts payable departments tried to discourage emailed invoices. We think the time has come to change that thinking. Here's why.

1. Emailed copies can be received much more quickly than mailed copies of invoices. For those with less than efficient processing, those extra days matter. What's more, even with the most efficient processes, you have no control over how long the post office takes to deliver a piece of mail. While they do a good job on most mail, there are always a few pieces that seem to take a vacation before landing in your office. By e-mailing invoices, you eliminate this problem.

2. If early pay discounts are involved, those few extra processing days are important. With suppliers getting increasingly diligent about either not offering early payment discounts or denying those that are taken after the discount date, every last day matters. Even one lost day can make a difference in many organizations.

3. If the invoice must be sent out for approval forwarding an email is pretty efficient compared with copying or scanning an invoice. If the supplier has emailed the invoice, no one in accounts payable has to spend time scanning it. It's like the vendor has done a portion of accounts payable's work and they don't charge for it.

4. If someone requests a copy of an invoice for research purposes, a copy can be forwarded without worrying

about documents being taken from files and not returned. With electronic documents, the old concerns about documents removed and either not returned or misfiled when they were returned are eliminated. Now, accounts payable can graciously share the document without having to act like the documents belonged in Fort Knox.

5. Emailed copies of invoices never get lost or damaged in the mail. Every company has received at least a few of those dreaded packages from the postal service containing invoices that were mangled during the mailing process. Inevitably, despite the postal services best efforts to get you the complete damaged document, parts of it are missing and you have to contact the supplier for another copy. That problem disappears with email.

6. Eliminate the need to open paper mail. Most accounts payable departments that receive invoices directly have someone who opens the mail and sorts the invoices. On a Monday this might take the entire day. On other days, a significant portion of the day might be eaten up by just opening the mail and sorting. This problem goes away with email.

7. PDF copies produced directly from the vendors computer are often easier to read than printed copies that may have been bent or crumpled in the mail. No longer do you have to squint and try and make out poorly printed documents or invoices that were squished in the mail.

8. When given the choice of a faxed invoice or an emailed copy, an email with a pdf attachment wins hands down all the time. You don't have to worry about the quality of your fax machine. What's more, many organizations are incorporating e-fax facilities into their fax process so

they never actually receive a paper document, only the email version of it.

We didn't talk about the benefits to the environment of receiving invoices electronically rather than by paper. Clearly there are benefits in that arena. For this article, we are simply focusing on the benefits to your department. Since we're going down this path, let's address the only complaint we typically hear when it comes to emailed invoices.

Some companies print the invoices once they receive them electronically. They complain about having to spend time and resources printing their supplier's invoices. We might suggest that the time spent printing is more than offset by the time saved opening and sorting mail. What's more, as the business community gets more accustomed to dealing with electronic documents, the need to print invoices will diminish and this argument will go away.

We believe electronic documents are the wave of the future and we all need to adjust to dealing with them instead of paper. What do you think?

Stopping Vendors from Sending Duplicate Invoices

It seems that every improvement bring its own set of problems. This is precisely what happened when more organizations began accepting e-mailed invoices. A growing number of vendors who e-mail invoices also send paper copies through the mail "just to be on the safe side." This of course creates extra work in accounts payable - not exactly the direction most organizations wish to go. We asked readers about the best ways to handle vendors who insist on sending invoices by e-mail and snail mail. What we found is there is no golden solution – but some of our readers were effectively dealing with the situation. What follows is a look at how they are combatting the problem.

The Basic Approach: Stopping the Duplicates

I personally haven't found a good way to get vendors to NOT send the original by snail mail and emailing a copy also, wrote several managers. Some of my vendors have been nice and not sending the original, but only by calling and begging them not to mail them if they email, points out one of them. Some are nice and some are not.

An Aggressive, but Effective Solution

Reject paper invoices, says a responding supervisor. She notes that one of the companies she worked for in the past wanted to work to achieve a 100% paperless environment, by accepting electronic invoices via EDI and e-mail. The organization had an aggressive notification campaign by sending letters to vendors, including letters in their checks, and also put a message on their remittance advice which covered vendors being paid electronically. They told the vendors that all paper invoices would be rejected and thrown in the trash.

There were some small companies that did not have the capability to send electronic invoices so there was a small percentage of paper still coming into the department but the list of vendors to process paper invoices was small. We should note that we heard from several e-invoicing software companies who pointed out that their products would solve the problem, weeding out duplicate invoices.

It's not only e-Mailed Invoices

Snail mail vs. email can certainly create issues, responded another manager, snail mail alone can still cause problems. A very large company with multiple well-known brand names always issues two invoice copies for each shipment, he explains. One invoice copy is enclosed with the shipment directly to the retail location (we operate 11 locations in 5 states), the other copy is mailed to our corporate PO Box.

This would be bad enough, except there is another issue. "All would be fine," he explains," except the invoice number shown on the mailed copy includes a series of leading zeros that do not appear on the ship-to copy. To help our Dynamics GP system reliably warns us of duplicate invoice numbers, our rule is to always add the leading zeros to this vendor's invoice number."

Dealing with the Issue

Given that it appears this is a problem that will be with us for some time, some of our readers have developed procedures to deal with it. They include the following.

1) We always send our requirement document to the vendors who ask about our electronic/emailed invoice option. It says, "Accounts Payable would love to partner with you on submitting invoices to us electronically however, please note our requirements for receiving invoices electronically at our invoices@.com mailbox."

- Only one invoice attachment per email is accepted.

- Accepted formats are PDF, Word, or Excel.

- Invoice number should be listed in the subject line to avoid documents combining into one.

- All invoices must contain a PO Number or Accounting Unit number and Full Name of person ordering product/service.

- No password protection or embedded links to obtain document can be sent.

- Only original invoices. No statements, past due or correspondence should be sent to this mailbox. Statements, correspondence, etc. should be sent to accountspayable@.com .

- Paper copies of invoices should not be mailed. This will become your invoice for payment.

2) To tackle duplicate invoicing in our organization, our software in Accounts Payable catches duplicate invoices

automatically. But, not everyone enters them the same way. If, for instance there are dashes within an invoice number, and it gets paid with the "dash" and another duplicate invoice gets mailed, faxed or emailed and it gets entered again this time without the dash, it won't catch. The solution was to bring this up in our on-going training sessions to enter invoice numbers exactly the way they appear on the invoice, including the dashes, letters before the number, example: INV12345. We ask our users to be consistent when entering invoice numbers and to follow the AP guidelines we have in place. So far, we have been successful in duplicating.

Concluding Thoughts

This issue will be with us for some time to come. The importance of best practices and duplicate payment checking continue. They are critical for identifying those duplicate invoices before they get paid. As time goes on and increasing numbers of invoices are sent electronically, perhaps this problem will diminish. But, for the present, stringent coding standards and standardized practices are critical for catching those problematic second invoices.

A 7 Step Game Plan to Weed out Duplicate Invoices

It would be nice if vendors would send one invoice and then wait for their payment. However, that doesn't always happen. When the payment isn't received by the due date, most vendors will send a second invoice. These are often not marked as a duplicate invoice or a copy of an invoice. It then falls to the accounts payable department to identify these unwanted seconds.

The Problem Gets Worse

Duplicate invoices have always been a problem. In the past they were typically sent only in the case of a late payment. That is now changing. Some vendors now send two invoices and this is creating massive headaches for the accounts payable staff who receive them.

There is an emerging problem of vendors emailing (or faxing) invoices and then for good measure because they want to make sure the invoice arrives, also mailing it as well. Whether the rationale for submitting the second invoice is devious or honest is irrelevant. It still means more work for accounts payable. That's why you need top-notch practices to identify these problematic second invoices.

The Game Plan

To deal with this issue, employing the following tactics will help identify and eliminate the duplicate invoices:

1) Identify those vendors sending by postal mail and e-mail and ask them to stop sending one of the ways. Occasionally, just asking vendors to stop sending multiple invoices solves the problem. However, many don't for a variety of reasons. Hence, it is critical to know who's doing this and utilize extra checking routines on these vendors.

2) Centralize the receipt of invoices. This ensures accounts payable knows of all invoices as early in the cycle as possible. It also makes it less likely that a duplicate will slip through.

3) Insist that the accounts payable staff processing invoices uses standardized routines and rigid coding standards. This means that everyone who processes invoices uses exactly the same procedures. It also means setting up a coding standard for everyone to use when entering data so all data is entered the same, regardless of who enters the information. This step is critical. If you don't employ this step it is likely that duplicates will slip through.

4) Strong internal controls from the moment the invoice arrives in your office until the payment leaves are also an important component in any approach to eliminate duplicate invoices. This should apply not only to invoices sent through the postal mail, but also electronic invoices, as well.

5) Create an Always-Check-Thoroughly (ACT) list of vendors who routinely submit duplicate invoices. This will

include not only those who submit through multiple channels but also those who are likely to send duplicates for other reasons.

6) Don't overlook the importance of staff training. When employees are first hired they should be trained by the most knowledgeable person available for the task. Periodically review their work to determine if additional training might be warranted. And, anytime a new process or procedure is introduced make sure everyone who might need it is given a thorough explanation of how the new process will work. Don't assume they will all figure it out. Also, update your policy and procedures manual with the new procedures so any employee who has questions can check on his or her own.

7) Don't overlook the benefits afforded by technology. With invoice automation, the task of identifying duplicates is a simple. Computers do an excellent job identifying duplicate invoices.

Concluding Thoughts

When all is said and done, sometimes despite the very best efforts of the accounts payable staff, a few duplicates do slip through and get paid. Unfortunately, rarely are those second payments returned by the vendors who received them unless they are nudged by the vendor or its representatives. That's why a payment audit is highly recommended as a last step in the process. It helps identify those cases where an extra payment was made. Payment audits should be part of every best-practice accounts payable function.

To ensure that the payment auditors find as little as possible, implement as many of the steps described above as you can before calling them in. That way, you collect the low-hanging fruit yourself and don't pay someone to do the easy work.

Chapter 3

The Business Community Takes a Giant Step away from Paper Checks: Electronic Payments

Without a doubt, the business community is finally moving away from paper checks. This move has been a long time coming. But, with consumers using online banking services in droves, it was only a matter of time before they started incorporating that practice in their business lives.

Making electronic payments in the business world is not quite as easy as it is for individuals. But once you have the process up and running, it will save your organization money on top of being more efficient for the payment function. Electronic payments in the US are handled through the Automated Clearinghouse (ACH); hence the term, ACH payment.

Because this issue is important, two chapters are devoted to it. This chapter addresses:

- How ACH Payments Work
- How to Start an ACH Payment Program
- The Importance of Remittance Information Issue
- The issue of Renegotiating Payment Terms
- How to Use ACH Payments to Solve the Rush Check Problem
- The issue of Replacing Wire Transfers with ACH Payments

How ACH Payments Work

People who get their paycheck directly deposited into their bank account are part of the electronic payment revolution. In fact, mimicking the direct deposit terminology that most people are familiar with, NACHA (the National Automated Clearing House

Association) recently named payments made electronically through the ACH "direct payments." NACHA, the Electronic Payments Association, is responsible for electronic payments that go through its local networks.

Automated Clearing House Network

The Automated Clearing House (ACH) Network is a nationwide batch-oriented electronic funds transfer system governed by NACHA. It provides for the interbank clearing of electronic payments for participating depository financial institutions. The Federal Reserve and Electronic Payments Network act as ACH operators, central clearing facilities through which financial institutions transmit or receive ACH entries.

NACHA represents more than 11,000 financial institutions through direct memberships and a network of regional payments associations, and 650 organizations through its industry councils.

ACH payments include:

- Direct deposit of payroll, Social Security and other government benefits, and tax refunds
- Direct payment of consumer bills such as mortgages, loans, utility bills, and insurance premiums
- Business-to-business (B2B) payments
- E-checks
- E-commerce payments
- Federal, state, and local tax payments

Most of what is written about electronic payments in this course will fall under the heading of B2B payments. The term electronic payments for the purpose of this course is synonymous with ACH payments.

For those readers who may want to peg their campaigns to grow their programs to some sort of a national initiative, May is Direct Deposit and Direct Payment month.

The Basics: ACH Credits

An ACH credit is a payer-initiated transaction. The payer instructs its financial institution to electronically transmit the payment through the ACH/Federal Reserve network to the payee's bank account. Typically the funds are available the day after the transaction takes place. This eliminates all delays associated with mail and processing float.

The most common examples of this are direct deposit of payroll, where the employer is the payer and the employee the payee. One of the biggest users of this type of payment vehicle is the Federal government when it direct deposits Social Security payments. In this case the recipients are the payees. It should be noted that starting in 2013, anyone signing up to receive Social Security benefits will have to receive them electronically. The Feds are starting to get out of the paper check business.

In recent years, businesses of all sorts have started making payments using the ACH instead of paper checks or in some cases, wire transfers. Because of the connection to direct deposit, this has led some to refer to this type of payment as a 'direct payment.'

The Basics: ACH Debits

An ACH debit is a payee-initiated transaction. The payee instructs the payer's financial institution to electronically transmit the payment through the ACH/Federal Reserve network to the payee's bank account. Typically the funds are available the day after the transaction takes place. These transactions are initiated using your bank transit and routing number and your bank account number. It is implied that you have given your consent but there is no formal verification process by the bank to ensure you have given your approval. There are new bank products just emerging that provide some protection against unauthorized debits.

The most common examples of the use of ACH debits is in the financial services sector. Some financial institutions granting mortgages will, with the payer's permission, debit the payer's bank account for the agreed amount on an agreed upon date each month. Sometimes there is a slight reduction in the mortgage rate in exchange for this arrangement. The insurance industry has also used this approach with some of its insurance products.

This payment vehicle has also migrated to the business community. Some states collect their sales and use tax using this approach. A few organizations make intercompany transfers this way. In a couple of rare instances ACH debits are negotiated as part of the terms and conditions in a sales agreement. While we never expect to see ACH debits play a prominent part in the payment world, they are a vehicle that will play a continuing role. It is critical that every professional involved with payments understand them because they are used by fraudsters in growing numbers.

Issues to Consider

As you are probably painfully aware, checks are costly and create lots of problems. Electronic payments are definitely cheaper—roughly 20 cents an item by most estimates—and create far fewer problems. Here are a few considerations to take into account when deciding to make the move away from paper:

- Float. Since the payment you initiate today will hit the payee's bank tomorrow, the mail and processing float are squeezed out of the equation. Some who find this objectionable, despite all the other savings, have renegotiated payment terms with their suppliers to make the transactions float neutral. For the most part, the float period is split. Since most people believe that mail and processing float is about five days, adding two or three days to the payment terms is generally considered acceptable. However, this should be discussed with suppliers rather than taken arbitrarily.

- Bank account reconciliations. Since there should be no outstanding items, bank account reconciliations should be easier for these items.

- Fraud issues. While a move to electronic payments will certainly reduce check fraud problems, it will not completely eliminate all payment fraud concerns. It would be naive to think that all fraud considerations would disappear. ACH fraud currently is at a much lower level than check fraud, but it does exist. Steps you can and should take to guard against ACH fraud. Note that some of these steps should be taken whether your organization makes electronic payments or not.

- Strong up-front controls. Since there is no signature on the payment, strong up-front controls are crucial as there is no signer "available" to catch errors. While it is true that signers shouldn't be catching mistakes, in reality they often do.

- Escheat. Since there are no un-cashed checks, there are no escheat issues related to payments made this way.

- Vendors. There are vendor issues related to cash application. While one would think that vendors would be clamoring to be paid electronically, this has not turned out to be the case. Apparently some systems have trouble applying cash received electronically. Thus, some of your vendors may be reluctant to accept payments electronically despite the obvious benefits.

- Staff reluctance to change. As with any new initiative, expect to find some of your staff dragging their feet and complaining about the change. It goes with the territory.

- Headcount. The reality is once your program is up and running, you'll need fewer people to process payments, if you've managed to convert a significant portion of your vendors to the process. However, don't jump the gun. Getting vendors on board to the electronic payment program will take time and effort. Thus, initially you may need more people if you want to make one big push. This is one of the reasons many organizations slowly add vendors to their electronic payment program.

How to Start an ACH Payment Program

New ACH payment programs will be started for a variety of any one of the following reasons:

- Someone in accounts payable or treasury recommends the vehicle. It can take several go-rounds before approval to start is received.
- Someone in management hears a talk on the benefits and comes back and orders accounts payable to start paying all vendors electronically.
- A key supplier asks your organization to pay it electronically.
- A key supplier demands you pay electronically if you want to continue buying from the company.

Benefits

The advantages of electronic payments are numerous. Lower cost typically heads the list of reasons organizations make the move. ACH payments are estimated to cost about 20 cents apiece while checks can range in cost from $3 to $20 (and sometimes more), depending on the process and efficiency of the issuing organization. Additional advantages include:

- Elimination of mailing costs.
- Supplier convenience through eliminating the check-cashing function.

- Simpler cash application process for the vendor when an e-mail with the pertinent details is sent along with the payment.
- No un-cashed checks means escheat issues are eliminated.
- Exception handling is minimized as errors are reduced.
- Accounting issues are also reduced.

The First Step

As with any high-level project, management buy-in is essential. Without management support, your program will fall apart as the complainers in your organization start whining. Even better than management support is a management evangelist, who fervently backs the program.

The cost savings associated with a program is a good way to get management support, as any savings offered by vendors for paying electronically go right to the bottom line. In fact, some organizations have used the program (at least initially) as a vendor benefit and asked for small discounts as a reward for paying electronically. Whether you will be able to do this will depend in large part on whether it is standard in your industry.

If you can't get support for the program, wait for the right opportunity. This might be when management calls for downsizing. Another opportunity might arise when a problem crops up that would not have occurred if you had the program in place.

It is also a good idea to make your bank your partner in this endeavor. As you launch the program, you will depend on the bank a great deal. Don't overlook this valuable resource.

Get input for your program from all affected parties, including likely critics. If you include them up front, they are less likely to cause problems down the road. In fact, if they feel they are part of the program, they may even advocate for it among other complainers.

Realize that it will be necessary to spend quite a bit of time coordinating the program at the start. Make a realistic assessment regarding information technology (IT) resources. Do you have the capability in-house, or will it be necessary to hire an outside service to get your program up and running? Even if the resources are available in house, will you be able to get an adequate allocation? What's more, if you get the allocation, do you expect the IT staff to be pulled off your project as more pressing projects arise?

Don't underestimate the effect instituting electronic payments will have on your staff. Getting vendors up and running takes time. Don't try to convert all your suppliers at once. Carefully estimate just how many vendors can be converted at one time. Better to have too few candidates in your first offering than too many.

Develop policies and procedures on how to make electronic payments from the accounts payable department. Make sure these processes are integrated into your entire payment process. This will mean involving purchasing and other accounting units. Some adjustments may have to be made in the accounting software to ensure that purchase orders (Pos) are canceled and checks are not cut when the payment is initiated.

A Good Starting Point

It's best to iron out the kinks in-house before testing the process on valued suppliers. You might require all payments to employees be made using the ACH. Be aware that while it is possible to do this for T&E reimbursements, some states do not allow organizations to mandate electronic payments for paychecks. Make sure to check your state requirements before trying this with payroll.

Perhaps some of your employees have been asking to be reimbursed electronically. If you want to start with a very small group to ensure the program is working, ask them to be your beta candidates.

To reduce calls from vendors or employees who don't know what the payments are for or don't realize they received it, provide e-mail notification capability, which may be linked to the vendor master file. This will mean getting e-mail addresses and keeping that file updated.

Third-Party Participation

When you are ready to invite participation, review your vendor listings. You might begin with those suppliers who have requested electronic payment in the past. You won't have to hold their hands as you walk them through the process. In fact, they may offer you some tips.

You might also consider those suppliers already being paid by wire transfer. They are accustomed to electronic payments, and the switch from wire to ACH will save your firm from paying wire transfer fees. Some organizations initiate wires outside the accounts payable process. Depending on your accounting system, ACH may tighten controls as all payments will go through one process instead of two.

When you are confident that you have everything under control, it's time to turn your attention to your suppliers. Once you are satisfied with the retooled program, roll it out to a small group. Get feedback again, and if necessary tweak the program to meet any objections and suggestions.

Make it easy for them to sign up. Send a letter to your targeted vendors including an ACH authorization form. Once again, start with a targeted list. The reason for this is simple: The response rate might be higher than you expect. If discounts are available from vendors for electronic payments, you will want to work with purchasing to ensure that you receive all you can.

Before Rolling Out to Your Entire List

Once you have a number of vendors enrolled, take a step back. Don't assume everything is going well; inquire if it is. Send an e-mail with your name and phone number to vendors included in the program. It is important to identify potential problems early in the game, when it is easier to fix them and not too many potential payees have been turned off by your process.

You should also anticipate problems. Talk to your peers at other companies and see what their experiences were. Here's a list of some problems encountered by professionals with active programs:

- Incorrect bank account information from suppliers
- Input errors
- Bank mergers resulting in changes to a bank's routing number
- Vendors failing to notify customers when closing or changing bank accounts
- ACH kickback notices not received
- Vendors not receiving e-mails with payment information

Vendor Participation

Identify what payments you want to include. If there is any chance that you will want to pay someone at some point with a purchase card (p-card), do not invite the vendor to participate in your electronic payment program. Here's why. When vendors receive a payment via p-cards, they must pay the bank a processing fee. This typically is between 2 and 3% unless the vendor is very small, in which case it might be higher.

Vendors that receive payments electronically will be extremely reluctant to accept credit card payments in lieu of electronic payments. Once this bell is rung, it is almost impossible to un-ring it. The only possible exception would be for very small payments, for which p-cards are ideal.

Break your target vendor list down into where you want to start and those payments and vendors who you might eventually want to include once the program is successful. Be aware that as word spreads, you may get requests to join your program. Remember also that if you are going to ask for a pricing discount, a small rebate or renegotiated payment terms, you will need to include purchasing, if that is the department that negotiates such issues with suppliers. This is a good way to improve relations with purchasing if they are frayed.

Also, once you get started, you may find that vendors who did not initially want to participate in your program will change their minds. Alternatively, another customer may have demanded they accept payments electronically and once they started, they find they prefer payments in this manner.

Be careful how you roll out your e-payment program. If you try to enroll too many vendors in at once, the program may blow up as you don't have adequate staff to handle it.

Document, Document, Document

When you introduce an e-payment program, your procedures will change. Update your policies and procedures manual, and share this information with all affected parties. If you have your procedures posted on your intranet site, add the new e-payment processes.

Not only will you have to write new procedures for the e-payment program, you may have to revise other sections that are affected by your new process. Do not overlook these.

This might also be a good time to review some of your forms used in the payment process and bring them up-to-date.

Train, Train, Train

With your new procedures in place, you will need to make sure the entire staff knows the new process. Never assume that the information is too basic. The accounts payable staff as well as anyone affected by the process, perhaps including purchasing and suppliers enrolled in the program, will need some training.

Without training, you could doom the program. Should one vendor have a bad experience, even if it was entirely the vendor's fault, you will have a hard time convincing that company to continue to participate in your program.

Once the program is up and running and you are ready to invite every vendor to participate, include an e-payment enrollment form with your new vendor pack and a welcome letter. Do not forget to ask for a voided check so you can verify the account number as well as the transit and routing numbers. Your vendor may offer a deposit ticket instead of the voided check. This will work most of the time. However, a few banks do not include the requisite information on their deposit tickets. Thus, if at all possible, get the voided check.

Don't Overlook Metrics

Most organizations adopt an e-payment program at least partially because of the cost savings associated with the process. Having promised management certain savings, it's a good idea to go back periodically and measure those savings to make sure the program is producing. It is also a good idea to do this so the next time you make a proposal and are asked about the savings related to ACH payments, you will not be blindsided.

The savings are not always that easily to quantify. At a minimum, they should include:

- Postage savings of not having to mail checks
- Check printing costs
- Check clearing costs at the bank
- Any discounts or rebates received from vendors for paying electronically
- Any headcount reductions that may occur as a result
- Time savings resulting from not having to process checks

Other savings may be unique to your organization. Include them. Of course, since you are including all the check-related costs, you will need to offset your savings with the cost the bank charges you for ACH payments.

Vendor Satisfaction Survey

Periodically, perhaps as part of a larger vendor satisfaction survey, ask participants in your program about their experiences. Take the results seriously, and tweak your program if the survey results indicate a weakness in your approach. Do not overlook the opportunity to ask participants for suggestions.

It is hoped that they will share with you approaches taken by other companies that work well—techniques you can incorporate into your own program. Use the survey to learn from your own mistakes as well as the success of others. There is absolutely no reason why if you see a good idea at another company you cannot bring it home and make it your own.

Concluding Thoughts

According to a recent Accounts Payable Now & Tomorrow survey, 73% of all organizations now make at least a few ACH payments. This is up drastically from 34% five years ago. Of the participants, 91% said they expected to be making payments through the ACH within five years. The number is probably understated. If you do not currently have an ACH program, begin investigating one. It's only a matter of time before the market will require it of you.

Don't Overlook the Remittance Information Issue

On the face of it, you'd think every supplier would be clamoring for electronic payments. Yet, some refuse to accept them. While at first this seems counterintuitive, there is a good reason for this reluctance. Their cash application folks have difficulty applying cash without that all important remittance information. If this hurdle can be overcome, many are all too happy to get onboard accepting electronic payments.

Create a separate e-mail with all the remittance information and e-mail it to the appropriate accounts receivable or cash application person at your vendors. This will provide them the information needed to apply cash correctly and should remove what is hopefully the last obstacle to their accepting electronic payments. What's more, if you are able to provide this information a day or two in advance of the payment, it might also help with their short-term cash forecasting—another side benefit.

If that's not possible, consider mailing the remittance information after the fact. While this is better than nothing, it does take away some of the cost savings associated with the move to electronic payments.

Ignore the issue of remittance advices and the number of suppliers willing to accept ACH payments will be lower than it might be otherwise. Even if your vendor is willing to accept payments electronically without remittance information, you are putting your organization at the mercy of their cash application person. Typically, without other instructions, they will apply whatever cash comes in to the oldest outstanding invoice. This may not be what you intended. For example it could be a disputed invoice that you have no intention of paying. Hence, it is critical that remittance information be included so the supplier knows precisely what you intended to pay with.

Renegotiating Payment Terms

Much has been written about renegotiating payment terms in this book. Often when the topic is raised, management is reluctant because they perceive that they will lose the float benefits. Companies that want to use this new technology yet are not willing to give up the few extra days of "float" can renegotiate their payment terms with vendors to make the transaction float neutral. This way neither party gains or losses by the transition to the new payment methodology.

When payments are made electronically, the funds get into the supplier's bank account immediately and generally the vendor has use of good funds one day later. This is typically several days sooner than if the check had gone through the traditional printing and mailing cycle. Recognizing this fact, some companies use this information to entice vendors to accept payments electronically.

Should you take this tack? In an ideal world the answer is, of course yes. But if vendors refuse to renegotiate the terms, you may end up continuing paying them with paper checks. So the real answer is: It depends. If your company's primary goal is to get rid of the checks, then the answer is to tread lightly on the float issue. If, however, cash flow is an issue for your firm, then you may have to rethink how you address the terms question. Accounts payable managers should not make this decision in a vacuum. Management input is required when deciding how important float is in this equation.

Pricing Discounts

Occasionally some suppliers will offer small pricing discounts or rebates to their customers who agree to pay them electronically. This is the best of all worlds for customers. They get to pay with the least expensive payment mechanism while simultaneously getting a price reduction or rebate—both of which effectively increase the bottom line. The offer of such savings has been more than enough to convince quite a few organizations to convert to electronic payments.

Like discounts offered for early payments, these incentives should be viewed positively and taken if at all feasible, assuming, of course, that they make financial sense.

Improved Terms versus Pricing Discounts

Generally speaking, the improved payment terms offered to make a transaction float neutral translates into two or three days added to the terms. Occasionally, if a vendor is very interested in getting paid electronically, it might offer an additional five days to make the transaction float neutral.

Pricing discounts, however, will generally be some fraction of 1%. Again, this is not a huge amount, unless you are talking about large invoices. However, it is found money that goes straight to the bottom line.

Although you should do the math if you are doubtful, generally speaking, pricing discounts or rebates should be taken, if offered, before the slightly extended payment terms.

If approaching the vendor to ask for an incentive, start with the pricing discount and then move on to the renegotiated terms to make the transaction float neutral.

Use ACH Payments to Solve the Rush Check Problem

A rush check (also referred to as an ASAP check) is any check produced outside the normal check production cycle. Organizations that run their checks from a mainframe computer are often forced to either use a typewriter or handwrite a check that is produced outside the normal cycle. Even those that print them on a personal computer have issues with rush checks.

Rush checks not only disrupt the work flow in accounts payable, making the department less efficient, they also open the door to fraud and duplicate payments. An inordinate amount of duplicate payments are checks that were rush checks. This is due to the fact that sometimes the check has been cut and is somewhere in the system, waiting for an approval, a signature, or to be mailed. Inevitably, both checks get cashed—and rarely is the second returned without the prompting of a duplicate payment audit.

The size of the problem will vary at different organizations depending on how good invoice processing procedures are and how accommodating the organization is toward requests for rush checks. Some organizations dig their heels in issuing rush payments only in cases of dire emergency while others allow them under almost any circumstance.

ACH payments provide a very real solution to the rush check dilemma. By adopting a policy that all rush payments requests that are honored will be fulfilled with an ACH payment, a company solves many of the problems caused by rush checks while simultaneously introducing new vendors to the electronic payment process. The vendor demanding the rush check will have good funds in its account before it would write a check. Often once a vendor experiences the benefits of ACH payments, it will willingly sign up for that type of payment in the future. It can be a win-win for both parties, turning a bad situation into one that improves supplier relations.

Replacing Wire Transfers with ACH Payments

For organizations that pay many obligations with wire transfers, the ACH alternative will save them a bit of money. This savings is often an added incentive to start such a program. Should you decide to replace wires with ACH, do not overlook the issue of availability of funds. Discuss it with each payee if you think it will be an issue. Most wires result in funds being available immediately, on the day the wire, for the recipient.

If you use the ACH, typically the funds are available the following day, although they should post on the day the ACH is done. This is similar to a check that might be deposited on one day but not be good funds for two or three days. If this timing is important, say in the payoff of a loan, you might have to initiate the ACH a day or two earlier. However, if the only concern is the date the funds hit the recipient's account, then there is no issue.

Universal Payment Identification Code

Even in this day and age, you will occasionally run into vendors who refuse to give you their bank account numbers so you can pay them electronically. They say they are concerned about their banking information being used fraudulently. Given the general concern about sharing banking information, it became apparent awhile back that a universal intermediary was needed. This was the genesis of UPIC.

A UPIC is a banking address used to receive electronic credit payments. A UPIC acts exactly like a bank account number; however, the UPIC protects sensitive banking information, that is, the bank account number and the bank's routing/transit number. The UPIC masks these numbers. Only credits to an account can be initiated with a UPIC. All debits are blocked, increasing security and control. Thus, a crook could not issue an ACH debit, write a check, or issue a demand draft.

If you are wondering if the UPIC can be used with wire

transfers, the answer, at least for the present, is no. Initially the UPIC may be used only in place of ACH credits.

Getting Started

If your vendors need instructions on how to get started, direct them to their bank. UPICs can be obtained from a participating bank. Most major banks will be able to facilitate this transaction. Contact your customer relationship manager or branch manager to find out if the bank issues UPICs.

It does not take long for the UPIC to be activated. Generally 24 hours after the application, the number will be live. It should be communicated with the universal routing and transit number (URT) for the bank. To be certain your vendor gets this right, the bank providing the UPIC should verify the URT.

You can find additional information about UPIC at https://www.theclearinghouse.org/payments/ach/risk-management/universal-payment-identification-code-upic

Closing Thoughts

Hopefully it is obvious by now that electronic payments are the way every organization should be paying its bills. If your organization has not started down this path, perhaps now might be the time to call in your banker to discuss what will be required to get going. But before you start make sure your own payment house is in order and that your upfront controls are up to snuff. If they aren't then perhaps that is where your focus should be. Once your controls are as tight as they can be, then start the discussion with your banker.

Chapter 4

Electronic Payments: Expansion and Innovation

Most organizations are aggressively looking for ways to improve their payment process. Making payments electronically is a huge first step in the right direction. But for it to make a meaningful difference, a company has to pay more than a few interested suppliers; they need to make a massive move in that direction. That doesn't happen overnight or without some serious efforts. In this chapter we examine:

- How to Expand an ACH Payment Program
- Tried and Tested Strategies That Convinced More Suppliers to Sign up for ACH Payments
- How to Avoid ACH Payment Conversion Nightmares
- ACH Best Practices
- The Hidden Surprises: The 'Gotchas' That Hinder ACH Success
- The Newest Developing Issue: Same Day ACH in the US

How to Expand an ACH Payment Program

You're convinced and you've even managed to get management on board. You all agree that paying electronically makes a lot of sense—both for you and for the suppliers you pay. Having won the internal battle, you now face your next challenge: getting an appropriate level of participation in the program. Not only does the program make financial sense for the company, but you've put your reputation on the line. How are you going to deliver?

Market Status

ACH payments alleviate many of the problems associated with paper checks. They are among the most cost-efficient payment mechanisms currently available. This is one of those issues that is actually win-win for both parties. Unlike other matters in business, where one party gains at the expense of the other, the automated clearing house (ACH) payment mechanism really does benefit both parties.

A few savvy vendors in aggressive markets will use ACH to develop a competitive advantage for their products. They do this in several ways. One technique currently in use is to offer slight pricing discounts or rebates to those customers who agree to pay them electronically. In cutthroat markets, this could give one supplier an advantage over another.

Another technique used is to renegotiate payment terms to make the transaction float neutral. Until recently, the request for the renegotiated payment terms came almost entirely from the customer. Now, in an attempt to entice participation, a few vendors are voluntarily offering slightly extended terms.

Don't think that because the vendor hasn't offered the pricing discount or renegotiated payment terms, they aren't available. Ask. Often vendors will grant them if asked; if not asked, however, they stay mum on the subject.

Methods to Grow Your ACH Program

Some strategies to raise supplier participation in your program follow.

- Don't bite off more than you can chew. Begin by figuring out how many suppliers you could comfortably convert from paper to electronic payment in a given month. There is a good reason to do this. If the response to your first offering is overwhelming, you may not be able to process in a timely manner everyone who expresses interest. The worst thing you could do for your new electronic initiative is not deliver as promised. If you fail with a particular supplier the first time out, it is going to be a long time before you get that supplier's agreement again.

- Start slow with a test group. These should be suppliers that either are already accepting payments electronically and/or those with whom you have a really good relationship—those vendors that won't be turned off if the first pass doesn't go as smoothly as you'd like. Vendors that have solicited you to pay them electronically make excellent candidates for your test group. Since they've requested you pay them electronically, they are more likely to be understanding if things go awry in the beginning.

- Roll out your program. Once you've figured out what you can reasonably handle and your processes are working smoothly, send out a mass mailing to targeted suppliers you want to pay electronically. You might, for example, exclude those suppliers you prefer to pay using the purchase card (p-card). Not everyone you solicit will accept your electronic invitation. So, if you can handle 100 conversions a month, send your initial solicitation to 200 or 300. Keep running your monthly solicitations until you have gone through your entire targeted market.

- Get on the phone. Once you've finished your initial campaign, you are ready to take the next, more aggressive, step. You'll need to go after the laggards who did not have the good sense to sign up for your electronic payment initiative. Begin by outlining all the benefits of receiving payments electronically. Once you have the list   firmly in hand, pick up the phone and start calling. Sometimes all it takes is a simple phone

call and a little conversation to get the ball rolling. At other times, the vendor will have a real objection; a real reason electronic payment cannot be accepted.
Address these issues if you can. If you can't, note what they are for future reference.

- If you can't get in the front door, try climbing in through a window. Now you have to get sneaky. The next time one of your nonparticipating vendors calls looking for a payment that was needed yesterday, take advantage of the opportunity. Even if the delay is entirely your company's fault, suggest that you can pay electronically today or tomorrow (whatever your schedule allows) but will not be able to draw a check and mail it until…. Point out that given mail time, it might take a week or more until the vendor has the funds in its account, but if you pay electronically, it can have good funds the next day.

- The door is never completely closed. After six months or even perhaps a year, revisit the issue with those who have not signed up. More often than not you will find that a vendor who did not have the capability when it was first suggested has upgraded, and you will be able to enroll a portion of this group.

- Roll up your sleeves and get ready to work. Now it's time to address the "problem children," the companies that have real operational issues that prevent them from accepting electronic payments. Go back to the notes you took when making your initial phone calls. Categorize them and identify the most common issues. Then look for solutions to those problems. See if any of the vendors you are currently paying electronically had these issues. If they did, find out how they solved the problem. Armed with this information, you are prepared to provide your suppliers with a potential solution. If the solutions you offer have some value, you may not only add the vendor to your electronic payment clients, but you will also have enhanced the relationship with that vendor—something purchasing should appreciate!

- Take a real hard-ball approach. This tactic won't work in every situation (especially if you are dealing with some 800-pound gorilla suppliers), but it will work on occasion. Levy a fee on those vendors who refuse to be paid electronically. Charge them $25 for every check you cut to them. (Note: Depending on the relationship you are trying to foster with your suppliers, this may not be a tactic you and your firm chose to employ. Accounts payable professionals should do this only with management's blessing and purchasing's knowledge. Should a key vendor complain, or, worse, halt deliveries, the repercussions from these two groups will not be pretty if they were not in the loop on this decision.)

- Don't overlook your Web site. Publish ACH information on the password protected supplier portal of your Web site, if you have one. Occasionally a vendor you might not have approached will want to participate. Make it easy. Also, if you are going to take this approach, include your vendor enrollment form on the site. Use this approach only if you are willing to include all vendors in the program. Otherwise, you may find your p-card vendors signing up for the program—and there goes your rebate.

- Vendor satisfaction survey. Include a question in your vendor satisfaction survey asking if the supplier would like to be paid electronically. Of course, do this only if you are looking to include that vendor in your program.

- Take advantage of those "where's my money" calls. When the vendor calls looking to ensure payment, (you know, those annoying calls vendors make to ensure you have the invoice and will be paying it on time) point out the benefits of receiving payments electronically and try and sign them up.

- Use your internal e-mail to promote the program. Take a page from the marketers' book. Develop a tag line for your e-mail messages that you send vendors. It could say something like "Interested in receiving your payments from us faster? Ask me about our electronic payment program."

- Cold call. Don't overlook the phone as a potential tool. Make sure you target the right person. Often the pitches go to the salesperson, who, in many cases, has little interest in the payment aspects of the transaction. Take your list of targeted vendors and start calling their accounts receivable or credit manager. These are the people who are likely to be interested in receiving payments electronically. If you are making the pitch on the basis of financial savings, you could also try the chief financial officer, controller, or treasurer.

- Universal Payment Identification Code (UPIC). Occasionally you will run into suppliers who are reluctant to share banking information for fear of fraud. Suggest they get a UPIC. UPICs are discussed toward the end of this chapter.

Tried and Tested Strategies That Convinced More Suppliers to Sign up for ACH Payments

The reasons for switching from paper checks to ACH payments are many. Cost, efficiency, minimization of unclaimed property issues and cash flow planning are just a few. Despite the recognized benefits to both parties, there is still some reluctance by many suppliers to accept electronic payments. AP Now, a boutique publishing, consultancy and training firm focused on accounts payable issues, recently asked readers of its free weekly e-zine who've been successful getting vendors to sign up for ACH how they persuaded them to do so. Here are a few of the better suggestions.

The Payment Frequency Issue

Perhaps the best way to get vendors on board is to pay less frequently with checks than with ACH. That's the strategy used by quite a few of AP Now's readers. Here are a few of their comments on implementing this tactic.

- To encourage ACH, checks were cut only twice monthly whereas we did ACH daily.
- Have quicker payment terms for those vendors that accept ACH payments.
- We encourage our vendors to give us a discount and be paid by ACH. We pay these vendors on a daily basis. Otherwise, they are paid once per week.

The Benefits Approach

Quite a few companies convince vendors by simply pointing out the benefits. Here's how a few of AP Now's readers addressed the issue.

- We just let them know that by accepting ACH payments, they get paid faster and with more accuracy. No more checks lost in the mail, having to void and re-issue checks, no more phone calls from vendors looking for check payments and being told they are in the mail. ACH are easier to provide proof of payment and to validate taking early pay discounts.
- We have stressed that the time it will take for the vendor to actually receive funds will be decreased by at least a week. Between mailing the checks, taking the deposit to the bank and waiting for the check to clear. If we send an ACH, they will have funds in their account within two business days.

- We were struck by a major tornado last April. Our facilities were not impacted but unfortunately several of our vendors' physical locations were. In addition to that, during the days after the tornado, mail service was slow, if available at all in some locations. Fortunately, many of our vendors had previously signed up for ACH and we were able to continue making payments to them during this difficult time. We have been able to use this as a "plus" for ACH to convince vendors who were not signed up for ACH to do so.

The Lost Checks Opportunity

A number of readers took advantage of checks lost either in the mail or by vendors to press for ACH. Here's a look at how a few of them handle the matter.

- We charge a replacement fee for lost checks unless the vendor has submitted an ACH request for future checks.
- Whenever a vendor calls to have a check voided and re-issued, we send them a form to sign up for ACH.
- Our company doesn't replace lost checks unless the vendor submits an ACH request.

A Helping Hand from Purchasing

Increasingly accounts payable's activities overlap with other departments, especially purchasing. Here's how two professionals recruited other departments to help.

- We encouraged the purchasing department, travel, premises (anyone engaging vendors to put ACH on the table as part of their negotiations). We managed to get some nice discount terms in the bargain.
- One of the strategies that our AP department implemented involves working in conjunction with our contracting team so that when it is time to renew our vendor price agreements, switching to electronic payment is part of the new contract.

Addressing the Remittance Information Issue

One of the biggest problems with getting vendors on board with electronic payments has to do with getting them the remittance information. Here's how two of professionals addressed that problem.

- Our company has a website where all the payments are posted (for a three year time frame) and the website also sends an auto email when the vendor has received a payment.
- Ask for an email address where remittance information can be sent.

Additional Strategies

Even after everything discussed, there are still a few more approaches being used by other companies. The first addresses vendor complaints about early discount payments received after the discount date and the second addresses the issue with new vendors. Here are the last two suggestions.

- We have some discount vendors still receiving checks. They will contact us requesting a discount be paid back because the check was not received in time. Our comment to this is we have no control over the mail time and suggest they switch to ACH. Allowing us to pay them by ACH they will receive our payments quicker and we will no longer have a late payment issue with discounts.
- Create a form that you can email over to all new vendors with their w9. Readers should verify information received on this form using contact information provided by the vendor.

Paying via the ACH is the wave of the future. It is much easier and less costly than paper checks. If you are looking for ways to increase participation (or get started) some of our proven tactics may be just what you need.

How to Avoid ACH Payment Conversion Nightmares

If you do not execute your ACH payment conversion carefully, you could end up dooming the program before it has a chance to start. Learning from others' mishaps is one way to avoid making the same mistakes yourself. Unfortunately, often people are not willing to share their horror stories. One such story is about an organization that had a terrible time converting vendors to receive ACH payment. Some of the issues that could have been handled better include:

1) Master vendor file. Not cleaning up the vendor database before requesting (actually demanding) that the vendors convert from check payments to ACH can lead to huge problems. One such organization had multiple active vendor codes in the system for the same vendors. It used SAP with one company code for multiple business areas.

A huge disadvantage to the one-code-for-multiple-areas method is that when a payment proposal is done for one business area, the vendor will rarely realize it was only for one business area, not the entire company. If, for example, vendor code 123 is in the proposal for business area ABC, when business area DEF runs its proposal, vendor code 123 will be blocked to them. SAP does not give you an error message or any type of notice that it has blocked certain vendors—you just have to be on top of it to know if you're expecting a vendor to be paid and it doesn't come up in your proposal.

That's a long-winded explanation, but it is the primary reason the example organization had so many active duplicate vendor codes. In addition, the method used for converting vendors to ACH was not very vendor friendly.

For example, Vendor ABC sells raw materials to eight of the firm's divisions. It had eight different vendor codes set up in SAP due to the blocking issue just described. A list of all of vendors and their addresses was obtained from SAP by business area. So the company had eight different lists, each one showing ABC once. As each list was processed separately, ABC received eight different requests (and threats) to send their banking information or else! A cutoff date was named after which the company would no longer be issuing checks to them.

Here's the kicker. ABC Company would say, "Mm, sounds pretty good, sign me up!" and fill out one of the forms. After all, it only has one bank account. ABC would send along a copy of the company W-9, which was also requested (not because it was needed for the ACH conversion, but to update records). This was probably the only thing the firm did right. The vendor would send back one form and one W-9. Each form had the vendor's number on it. The company only updated the one vendor number that was on the one form ABC sent back—not all eight vendor numbers. Therefore, one vendor code was changed to ACH, the other seven received a threatening second request letter (which they ignored since they thought they had already responded) and continued to receive check payments until the company put them on payment block and quit paying them altogether. You can imagine how well this went over.

2) Getting accurate bank information. Another big mistake was not requiring a copy of a canceled check to enter the ACH information from. The company accepted handwritten forms. This is a huge no-no. First, people get ACH payments and wire transfers confused. To the vendors, they are one and the same. To the banks, they are not. Many people gave the American Bankers Association (ABA) routing number for wire transfers and the ACH payment was rejected which wreaked havoc on the company's computer systems. The staff spent many frustrating hours on phone calls trying to explain the difference to people only to wind up calling their banks in the end anyway.

3) Fraud potential. The company was also often fearful of the following scenario—one that could be avoided simply by asking for that voided check. After setting a vendor up on ACH payment (from a handwritten form with an illegible signature), the vendor would call and ask why the company had stopped paying them. After further investigation, the staff would discover that the account the company was sending money to

did not belong to the company at all, but to a disgruntled mail clerk who had left the company shortly after completing the form with an offshore account set up in an untraceable alias. You should insist on getting a voided check.

4) Vendor setups. Another mistake was that after going through all this work to clean up vendors, change accounts, and update records, the company did not centralize vendor setups to one individual who was responsible for verifying and maintaining data. It simply changed its procedures to require all new vendors to accept ACH payment in order to be set up in the system, but the procedure was not enforced.

Vendors that had been blocked for noncompliance were gradually unblocked, and the amount of checks issued began to rise. Without one central department being held accountable for the integrity of the vendor database, the entire effort of the ACH conversion project was completely wasted.

While it is never possible to completely eliminate all problems, use the procedures that follow will make a big dent in the problems you will encounter when starting an ACH payment program—especially if you insist that all your vendors participate:

5) Get banking data from a voided check—not a handwritten form.

6) Request an up-to-date W-9 at the same time.

7) Start your electronic payment program with a small group so you can make adjustments to your program before rolling it out to your entire vendor constituency.

8) Before you demand that all vendors accept payments electronically, make sure all your systems and processes are working 100%.

9) If one vendor is in your master vendor file more than once, make sure those entries are linked for purposes of updating with banking information.

ACH Best Practices

With the drive on everywhere to move from paper to electronic payments it is important that best practices are integrated into the new payment process. For without best practices, fraud and duplicate payments will creep back in. What follows is a list of best practices every organization should use for ACH payments

Best Practice #1: Have detailed written procedures for your ACH program and include them in the AP policy and procedures manual. Don't assume your staff knows what to do.

Best Practice #2: Make sure your ACH procedures mirror you check procedures. It is critical that when processing invoices, the organization continue using the same best practices, strong internal controls and segregation of duties as is used when paying with paper checks. For if any of these steps are omitted, the organization would unintentionally weaken controls and incur other problems.

Best Practice #3: Integrate strong internal controls throughout the process. Make sure that when the ACH process is set up, no control point is overlooked. This includes making sure that appropriate segregation of duties is maintained.

Best Practice #4: Check for duplicate payments made using other payment methodologies, i.e. paper check, T&E and p-card. Ideally every organization should be paid using one and only one payment mechanism. More than occasionally, ACH payments are made outside accounts payable and the department making the payments does not employ the same rigorous practices used in accounts payable. When this happens and an invoice shows up in accounts payable, the accounts payable staff will pay it, as they cannot tell from the records that the payment has already been made.

Best Practice #5: Make sure receivers and POs are extinguished just as they would be if a paper check was the payment mechanism. This is probably the biggest potential problem spot when payments are made outside accounts payable. So, not only should the three-way match be done by whoever is making the payment, it is critical they extinguish the receiver and PO. If they don't do this, accruals and financial statements will not be accurate, as well.

Best Practice #6: Put ACH blocks on all accounts where ACH activity will not be allowed. This is something every organization should do, regardless of its participation in the electronic payment arena. For without it, an account takeover is made just a little bit easier for the crook.

Best Practice #7: Use ACH filters on those accounts where ACH debit activity will be allowed. This limits the activity to those who you have given permission to. Please note that the filter only checks for allowable parties; it does not review whether the transaction in question has been approved nor does it look at dollar amounts.

Best Practice #8: Have daily bank account reconciliations done on all accounts where ACH blocks are not used. Even better, reconcile all bank accounts on a daily basis. This ensures you are able to identify unauthorized ACH transactions within the 24 hour window, discussed earlier. The bank reconciliations have to be done anyway, so why not do them in a manner that will enable you to catch a fraud while something can still be done about it.

Best Practice #9: Use a separate PC for all your online banking activities and do not use the computer for anything else. Given the low cost of PCs, there's no reason why everyone isn't doing this.

Best Practice #10: Keep up to date on the latest information regarding fraud protection products offered by your financial institution and new frauds being perpetrated by crooks. They are getting amazingly creative. This is just one more area where it is imperative that every organization have the very latest information.

The Hidden Surprises That Hinder ACH Success

Speeding up cash disbursements isn't an approach most organizations willingly adopt. It's even worse when the move is unexpected—something that somehow never happens when the organization is flush with cash. (It always seems to occur when cash is tight.) Yet, that is exactly what can happen when an organization moves from checks to ACH if they don't plan ahead and make the appropriate changes in payment terms. Whenever an organization makes a change in procedures, it is crucial that thought be given to all the ramifications; the move to ACH is no exception. AP Now recently asked readers of its ezine who've made the move to ACH what issues others should expect so they can avoid fallout.

Extinguishing POs and Receivers

One of the first issues that come to mind is a surprising metric. While most checks payments are made through accounts payable, the same cannot be said for ACH payments. In a good number of organizations ACH payments are also initiated in other departments.

A very real concern is that the other departments might not extinguish the POs and open receivers opening the organization to another potential avenue for duplicate payments. We believe if others are to make ACH payments, it's crucial that adequate training be provided to those individuals. Open POs and receivers can result in duplicate payments should a second invoice be presented.

Additionally, state auditors could construe the open receiver as unclaimed property. And, if you think this is something I'm making up, let me warn you that a few organizations are fighting with state auditors over this very issue right now. Should the auditors win, they will be looking at every organization's open receivers when they come for an audit.

Open receivers can cause a misstatement of your financial records if those receivers are used for accrual purposes. If there are enough of them, the misstatement could be material. This is something no one wants hanging over them.

Obviously these issues are avoided if the firm insists that ACH payments must flow through the accounts payable system.

Setup Time Involved

"Our ERP software for the pay cycle was setup to create ACH files from these invoices but the output was nothing like what was required from the bank," reports an AP manager who requests anonymity. She notes that her staff spent endless hours completing the process to automate ACH payments. The company cut ACH payments for over 30 companies and all activity is now output to a file that is uploaded to its bank once a day. While the time savings once the process was in place is impressive, underestimating the time and effort needed to get the ACH process up and running can come back to haunt you.

This company was not home free once they had the process working, however. When they merged with another organization, they had to integrate their ACH payments with their new partners'. In this case the treasury department was involved and coordination became an issue.

Cash Flow Implications

Changing to ACH has a direct and immediate effect on cash flow. "ACHs clear the next day while your checks require mail time and deposit time at the bank, which could leave the funds in your account anywhere from three to ten days," points out an accounts payable/receivable manager.

One way to compensate for the immediate disbursal of funds, she says, would be to extend your payments to vendors a few days longer. So if you would normally cut a check on, say, May 16th wait until the 22nd to make the ACH payment. In fact, many organizations anticipate the cash flow impact and renegotiate terms with their vendors at the time they move to ACH. Those who ignore this issue will have a rude awakening the first time the ACH payments hit.

Depending on how tight the cash flow is in your organization, this could be the worst problem of all and the one with the highest visibility. If the company runs out of cash and the cause of the liquidity crisis is identified as the move to ACH without an accompanying renegotiating of payment terms, the results will not be pretty. This is *not* how any employee wants to come to the attention of upper management.

The Cash App Issue

As discussed above, the remittance advice can be problematic since there is no check stub for the vendor to see what invoices are being paid. Another manager prints off remittance advices and e-mails them to the vendors. She notes she could mail it but the payment would arrive before the remittance advice. She also points out that when vendors don't know how to apply payments, they call. And that adds more work to the accounts payable department partially offsetting the productivity gains from going electronic.

Finally, if the remittance advice is mailed, the postage cost savings goes up in smoke.

Concluding Thoughts

Use of the ACH for payment processes can result in significant savings for the organization. However, like any new process, if the full ramifications are not explored its implementation can make the process worse rather than better. By addressing the issues discussed above, you will be well on your way to avoiding an ACH implementation debacle.

Developing Issue: Same Day ACH in the US

Modernizing the US payment system in a manner that creates value for both the end users and the banks is one of the reasons for the move to same day ACH. The new rules reflect the original proposal with a few minor, but important, changes. You can see them listed further on in this chapter. When the changes are all implemented businesses and consumers will have the choice of speed. Let's take a look at what's coming in the payment arena.

What the New ACH Will Look Like

The ACH network will establish a new option for same-day clearing and settlement via the ACH. Until now, in the US, the only way to accomplish this was to send a costly wire transfer or hand over cash. The last was really not an option in the corporate world.

Under the rule, two new same-day settlement windows will be added to the ACH Network, increasing the movement of funds between financial institutions from once a day to three times a day. Additionally, the receiving institution must provide faster funds availability to its customers, albeit at a cost. The methodology for calculating the fee that may be charged was also provided.

A Phased in Approach

The proposed changes will not all go into play at once. Some have wondered why not make all the changes at once. NACHA had surveyed its members and based on the feedback from that survey, decided to implement in this manner. Spreading implementation across three phases will ease the industry's implementation effort, and allow the industry to acclimate to a faster processing environment with same-day ACH credits prior to processing same-day ACH debits.

The decision to start with ACH credits was made because they have fewer exceptions and returns than do ACH debits.

Changes will be phased in in three steps as follows:

Phase 1: ACH credit transactions will be eligible for same day processing. This is meant to support hourly payroll, person-to-person payments and same-day bill pay.

Phase 2: Same day debits will be included. This is meant to support a wide variety of consumer bill payments, including but not limited to utility, mortgage, loan and credit card payments.

Phase 3: Faster ACH credit funds availability requirements for the receiving financial depository institutions will be introduced. Funds from same day ACH credit transactions will need to be available to customers by 5 PM local time (at the receiving institution's location).

Some Additional Questions

Here are the answers to some additional questions that many professionals are asking about this new process.

1) What's eligible for same day ACH? Both ACH credits and debits will be eligible for same-day processing. Only international transactions and high-value transactions above $25,000 would not be eligible for same day ACH.

2) What are the clearing and settlement times? There are two:

- A morning submission deadline at 10:30 AM EDT, with settlement occurring at 1:00 PM.
- An afternoon submission deadline at 3:00 PM EDT, with settlement occurring at 5:00 PM.

3) What are the effective dates for each phase?

- Phase 1 becomes effective September 23, 2016;
- Phase 2 becomes effective on September 15, 2017;
- Phase 3 becomes effective on March 16, 2018.

These dates are contingent upon receiving timely commitment from the Federal Reserve to support the Rule, which is necessary to ensure that same day ACH is ubiquitous across all 12,000 financial institutions in the US.

4) What will happen if an organization tries to make a same day ACH transaction for more $25,000? The ACH operator will change it to a next day ACH.

5) Why are international transactions excluded from same day transactions? International transactions, as many readers are aware, have to be screened against OFAC lists. This additional requirement would make it difficult, if not impossible, to meet the time deadlines imposed for same day transactions.

6) If we are making Rush payments by wire transfer, will same day ACH provide a cheaper alternative? Only in some cases will same day ACH replace wire transfers. Remember, there is a

$25,000 limit (at least for now) on all same day ACH items.

The Changes from the Original Proposal

1. The morning same-day window was modified to allow for more time to process transactions, with settlement occurring at 1:00 PM EDT.

2. The rule creates an option for an additional method for originating depository financial institutions to use, at their discretion, with their originators to determine intent for same-day settlement.

3. There was an adjustment to the methodology for calculating the Same Day Entry fee to exclude opportunity costs from its calculation.

Concluding Thoughts

Keep in mind that same day ACH may only be the next step in a move towards faster payments. There are likely to be other innovations coming down the pike. Many bankers question the advisability of building the same day functionality into the current ACH network. They do not necessarily believe that the batch processing, which underlies the current ACH system, is the best approach. However virtually all concede that same day ACH is inevitable. AP Now agrees with them on that call.

If you think your organization might want to take advantage of same day ACH, begin discussions with your bank sooner rather than later. There are likely to be new file submission requirements, cut-off times, exception resolution cut-off times and deadlines. The banks are scrambling with this just as the corporate world is, so there may be some hiccups along the way and your bank might not have all the answers you need as quickly as you like. So, be prepared to be patient and work with the bank. The end result will be worth the effort.

Clearly this is a big change to the way US payments will be handled.

Chapter 5

Expense Reimbursement Receipts: The Bombshell Issue Many Don't Expect

Not everything in the business world progresses the way you think it would. This is certainly true when it comes to the travel and entertainment (T&E) expense reimbursement process. Who would ever think the IRS takes a more liberal stance on some issues than the corporate world. But, that is exactly what has happened with the receipt issue. In this chapter we examine:

- The Changing Face of the Expense Reimbursement Process
- How Companies Just Like Yours Now Handle the Expense Reimbursement Process
- Changes in Receipt Requirements when Asking for Expense Reimbursement
- Why Some Companies Are Starting to Get Meal Receipts

- The Detailed Meal Receipt: How They Help Run a Tighter Reimbursement Function
- Scanning Receipts: Dealing with the Two Main Problems

The Changing Face of the Expense Reimbursement Process

Expense reimbursement procedures for employees travel and entertainment expenditures are a necessity for every organization. While you might think this function is static and once you have good policies and procedures in place, your organization is set for life, this unfortunately is just not the case.

Like almost everything else related to accounts payable, the expense reimbursement function is impacted by new technologies and regrettably, new frauds. Let's take a look at what's going on in the expense reimbursement space.

New Features

· Perhaps the most innovative upgrade we've seen in the products offered by third party service providers relates to the automated mileage checker. Several of the service providers' expense reimbursement products automatically check the mileage reimbursement requests submitted by employees.

While it is true that savvy professionals have been getting online and verifying mileage reimbursement requests using mapquest and other online sites that provide driving directions, some of the service providers have automated this process.

· Possibly the biggest innovation in this arena has been the move to a Software-as-a-Service SaaS model. This has brought automated expense reimbursement processing and verification into the realm of affordability for middle market companies.

It also allows for 100% verification – something that is not recommended in a manual processing environment due to the cost of doing so. With this dramatically lowered cost of entry, automated expense reimbursement processes are now within the financial reach of most organizations.

· The last change that we've observed is the inclusion of expense reimbursement processing in some of the e-invoicing models currently available on the market. This means that some of our readers will have access to automated expense reimbursement processing at no additional cost.

We'd like to note that automated expense reimbursement means more checking and unfortunately possibly more unpleasant surprises.

New Problems

As mentioned to above, there have been some new problems in the expense reimbursement arena we didn't have in the past – and we can't blame them all on technology. Culpability for the first, however, can definitely be placed at technology's feet.

Employees are now taking pictures of their receipts with their smartphones. This is a big plus as it definitely gets rid of the paper. However, many (not just a few) readers have reported the submission of cell phone copies of receipts multiple times.

Whether this is accidental or the employee is trying to defraud the company is irrelevant when it comes to addressing the issue. Without a doubt, additional resources will be needed to check and verify receipts. In some cases, audits may not be a bad thing either.

The next technology-induced problem relates to gift cards being included on the bill for a legitimate business reimbursable meal. While it shouldn't be necessary to mention that this is not acceptable in the organization's Travel & Entertainment policy, it might not be a bad idea to prohibit this. Requiring detailed meal receipts along with the receipt showing the total expenditure including the tip is the best way to protect the organization against this type of fraud. Hopefully, your employees will be smart enough not to include a receipt showing the purchase of a gift card.

Finally there is the issue of all those extra fees airlines now charge. They range from the reasonable to the ridiculous – and need to be addressed. Some organizations already address in their travel policy the issue of how many checked bags are allowed. Those who don't address the issue of checked bags in their policy might want to consider doing so.

Some airlines now charge extra fees for boarding early, having the airline select your seat ahead of time, printing your ticket at the airport and my favorite, for use of overhead compartment for storing a carry-on bag. Expect to see an increase in these fees on your employees' expense reports.

Technology Eliminates an Old Problem

One of the biggest thorns in the side for those reviewing expense reports are all those cash expenditures with questionable handwritten receipts. Perhaps the biggest potential weak spot is those cab rides documented only by a small slip of paper with figures filled in by the employee. Today, it seems every small business owner takes credit cards, thanks to the wide dispersion of devices that hook to a smart phone and use wireless Internet connections to verify credit card account information.

Most cab owners in cities where credit cards are not taken in taxi cabs now have this technology. Because of this there should be a dramatic decrease in the number of taxi rides paid for in cash. While this may not make the cab owners happy, it is good news for organizations whose employees travel.

Insist on use of p-card for all expenditures. Require that exceptions be documented separately. Clearly cards can't be used for tips for services provided by bellman and for the maids who clean up hotel rooms; that should be the extent of expected cash expenditures spent by business travelers.

Closing Thoughts

Two simple best practices will close many of the loopholes that facilitate the games some employees play with their expense reports. Require that the detailed meal receipt be submitted for any business meal and insist on use of a corporate card for any reimbursable business expense wherever possible. Yes, there will be exceptions – places where cards can't be used. But they should be few and far between.

As a side benefit, we expect a small drop in the total spend shown for business meals. When employees know they have to submit the receipt showing what was ordered, they may think twice before ordering that $50 appetizer or that   third bottle of expensive wine.

Travel & Entertainment: The Receipt Issue

Accounts Payable Now & Tomorrow (www.ap-now.com) recently conducted a survey to determine what companies were doing with regards to their receipt requirements for employees seeking reimbursement for expenses incurred while traveling. The results were not at all what we were expecting.

Highlights

1) Almost 60% of all companies require receipts for all travel and entertainment reimbursement requests made by their employees – regardless of the dollar amount involved.

2) Smaller companies, those with fewer than 250 employees, are only slightly more likely to require receipts than their larger counterparts.

3) The most anticipated change coming to the T&E receipt requirements is the requirement that the detailed meal receipt be turned in with all reimbursement requests for meals. The charge on this front is being led by midsize companies, that is those with 251 – 1000 employees, where 41% are considering this change. This number might have been higher but for the fact that numerous respondents indicated they already require the detailed meal receipt.

4) While only a few companies are considering changing the amount level at which they will require receipts, about twice as many are contemplating lowering it as compare to those thinking about raising it. Only 10% in total are envisaging a change.

5) When asked if they were concerned about employees eating an inexpensive meal and then putting in for reimbursement request just under the level where a receipt is required, only 25% indicated this was an issue for their organization. However, when you consider that 60% already require receipts for everything, this implies that 85% have some issues in this area.

Metrics from the Survey

Survey Participants

- Smaller Companies (those with fewer than 250 employees) 36.5%
- Midsize Companies (those with 251 – 1000 employees) 27.0%
- Large Companies (those with over 1000 employees) 36.5%

Receipt Requirements

- We require all receipts 58.90%
- $5 0.61%
- $10 1.23%
- $25 26.38%
- $75 3.68%
- Other 9.20%

Do you have a different receipt requirement for meals?

- Yes 30.06%

- No   69.94%

Are You Considering Any of the Following?

- Increasing the level where receipts are required   6.79%

- Decreasing the level where receipts are required   3.09%

- Requiring a detailed receipt for meals showing

    exactly what was ordered   26.54%

- None of the above   50.62%

- Other please explain   12.96%

Commentary: Most in other category already require detailed receipt. A few considering move to per-diems.

The Receipt Game Question

In some organizations there is concern over employees eating an inexpensive meal and then putting in a reimbursement request just under the level where a receipt is required. Is this a concern in your organization?

- Yes   25.31%

- No   74.69%

A Sampling of the Ridiculous Reimbursement Requests

When AP Now asked survey participants if they'd be willing to share the most ridiculous reimbursement requests they'd ever encountered, we didn't expect the outpouring we received. We ended up with seven pages of short vignettes. Rather than overwhelm this short paper with them, we've selected a few – and the decision which to include was a difficult one. We'll share additional ones throughout the year in our free weekly ezine.

Sign up box on the top left of www.ap-now.com

Here are some of the survey respondents' stories, in their own words:

- As far as meals go, we had one individual reporting business dinners on Friday nights. He had the company name and guest names. His approver finally decided that they did not do business on Friday nights and he contacted the restaurants and asked for detailed receipts - something at the time we did not require. Well the one meal was a table of four including two kiddie meals! We now require detailed receipts for anything over $40 so things like this can be caught.

- Conference in France, per receipts dates, times, locations, could see they toured France during the times they should have been attending the conference. The person also requested reimbursement for cigarettes on gas receipts. Fortunately, we had a French dictionary and a map of France.

- Request for reimbursement of pet-sitting expense while on a business trip.

- Individual purchased numerous items of clothing on a trip because he didn't realize they dressed up in that office, including shoes for $425.

- Luggage needed for traveling.

- Helicopter ride in Hawaii while at a conference.

- Due to a manager recently moving and having to take some unexpected trips it was agreed we would pay for his dog's kennel fees because he did not have family or know anyone in the area. The employee then proceeded to have the 'royal treatment' for his dogs including 'spa treatments'. Needless to say we only paid the boarding fee.

- We require itemized meal receipts and someone forgot to get one so they took a picture of the chicken wings they ordered and submitted that as their receipt.

- 12 beers and one order of Buffalo wings to 'discuss' the professional future of a direct report - only 2 persons on the meeting.

- We had one applicant list gummy bears, beer, and flowers on his expense report for his interview trip. Needless to say, we deducted all these charges. To my surprise, despite the frivolous expenses, he was actually hired!

- The individual did not have the receipt so they attached a copy of the menu from the restaurant and circled the items that were eaten.

  Editor's Note: Who said life wasn't stranger than fiction? I couldn't make this stuff up if I tried.

Change in T&E Receipt Requirements when Asking for Expense Reimbursement

You would expect that companies changing their receipt requirements for expense reimbursements would raise the dollar level where receipts are required. New research from Accounts Payable & Tomorrow shows just the reverse. Very few are taking that action. What's more, quite a few are asking for more details. Let's take a look at what the survey revealed.

Changes Being Considered for T&E Receipts

While half of the respondents aren't considering changing the receipt level, the other half are. This in and of itself is significant because it signals that many organizations are looking at the issue. While the IRS only requires receipts for expenditures in excess of $75, very few companies have followed their lead. Most use a lower dollar level. When evaluating the numbers below, please keep in mind that almost 60% require receipts for everything, regardless of the dollar level.

Action Being Considered	% Considering
Increasing the level where receipts are required	6.79%
Decreasing the level where receipts are required	3.09%
Requiring a detailed receipt for meals showing exactly what was ordered	26.54%
None of the above	50.62%
Other please explain	12.96%

We were intrigued to learn what other changes readers were considering and we thought you would be too. They are:

1) Itemized receipts required when eating with others.

2) Requiring additional receipts for charged items. Credit card statements are sometimes vague.

3) Per Diems. It should be noted that a number of respondents reported they were considering this move. The beauty of it is it eliminates lots of checking and other issues.

4) Having lower thresholds for receipts for newly hired employees.

5) Detailed receipts for meals.

6) We are looking at both a per diem option and also requiring the itemized meal receipt.

The Ugly Issue

In some organizations there is concern over employees eating an inexpensive meal and then putting in a reimbursement request just under the level where a receipt is required.

Respondents were asked if this was a concern in their organization.

Keep in mind, that almost 60% are already requiring a receipt for everything. Even with that, 25.31% are troubled by this issue.

The Even Uglier Issue

Lastly we asked respondent, if you are willing to share, how their organization treated inappropriate expense reimbursement requests. Whether it's the impact of a poor economy, a better understanding of how poor expense reimbursement habits hurt the bottom line or a fear of the IRS is not clear. But, overwhelmingly the tide seems to be turning. Finally, there appears to be overwhelming management support when it comes to dealing with questionable expense reimbursement requests.

There were over 100 responses to this question so we'll summarize to some extent. The most common response was that the expense was simply denied. One participant summed it up this way; "One word...no!"

Some simply took it off the expense report and reimbursed them at the lower amount while others sent it back asking the traveler to resubmit. Many copied the traveler's supervisor when they took this action. The next common approach was to return the offending report to the supervisor who had approved the item asking them about it. There were many variations on how this is done, but here's one explanation that was typical of our respondents. "The expense report form is returned to the manager who approved it with a copy of the company policy & procedure for expense reporting. A brief note on what the issue is would be noted."

Referencing the travel policy is a common tactic even for those who deny the reimbursement request outright. Many noted how they were able to do this because they have a strong travel policy and are backed by management on this issue.

Additionally, many counsel the employee.

Here are some other strategies used by the survey participants worth consideration. Virtually all of these were mentioned by several respondents.

1) Referred to finance supervisor and then to the employee's immediate supervisor for review and discussion with employee.

2) Since the expense report has to be approved by the manager before being submitted to Accounting, we bring up questionable receipts to the manager and have them obtain the answers from their employee. Most times, the expenditure gets removed before being resubmitted.

3) Expense is rejected by AP any appeal must go through the CFO. Not surprisingly, few choose to take this route. Escalate the situation to Corporate and Internal Control in order to evaluate situation and include it on an special log, Fraud revision, review the policy to identify any necessary update or change and take any necessary action with employee."

4) A warning e-mail is sent and a discussion with CFO ensues.

5) They are taken to the partner of the group, the situation explained and then the employee is made aware that they will not be reimbursed for the charges, and warned not to try again.

6) Discussion with employee and supervisor who signed off on it.

7) Kick it back to the approver and have them either confirm in email, or approve by signature a statement that they are aware of the expense being outside the

T&E policy and give a reason why they are approving it anyway... noting that it is a an 'exception'.

8) We forward the reimbursement request to our VP of Finance who usually denies the request.

9) Do not reimburse them for the most part. If we do they are considered taxable income.

10) If an employee out and out lies, he or she could be and have been terminated.

Not Always a Bed of Roses

Now if you've been reading the comments above and wondering if your organization is the only one NOT supporting its accounts payable staff when it comes to ludicrous expense reimbursement requests, the answer is no. There were a few respondents who did not get the support demonstrated by the commentary above. But, we must be honest. The number of professionals not getting full support on this issue is dwindling and is probably under 10% at this point. Here are a few responses from those who are not getting any backing.

1) Senior Management is asked to review and provide their approval. They almost always approve.

2) We don't get any backing from Executives on questionable expenses so we end up reimbursing everything. It's quite frustrating.

3) They are reviewed by upper management who has the final say in whether or not it will be reimbursed. I have been shocked when some requests are actually denied. Typically the person in upper management lets the individual know it will be paid as a one-time exception.

4) Depends on the level of the fraudster. Directors and above, it would be suicide to question, although we have brought it to our supervisors attention. Below that level we go after the supervisors to crack down, or we just adjust obvious fraud.

5) This is handled on a case by case basis. Our company is frustrating for the accounting department. They allow Managers to override and approve, which they do for the employees they like. They then ask AP and Accounting why there is such variance to Budget

Since expense reimbursement is a top IRS issue, we expect this topic to continue to be of interest to our all professionals interested in expense reimbursement best practices.

Why Some Companies Are Starting to Get Meal Receipts

Processing and auditing travel and entertainment expense reimburse requests is tedious enough without adding another step. But that is exactly what some organizations are starting to do. They are requiring the meal receipt that shows exactly what was ordered. While a few companies have been doing this for years, most haven't. What follows is a short list of the reasons why these receipts are sometimes requested and then a discussion on the best way to handle this additional influx of paper (or hopefully images to be audited).

The Rationale

If you are scratching your head wondering why receipts are being requested, consider the following.

1) If your organization has grants that prohibit the use of the funds to pay for alcohol, you might want require this additional documentation. Additionally, a few companies do not reimburse for liquor for individual meals so they might also wish to monitor. By the way, this is not to say that your employees cannot have a drink with their meals. They simply

must pay for it themselves. This means either requesting a separate bill or deducting the amount from the reimbursement. In an era when organizations need to keep costs under control, making sure that spending outside the approved policy does not occur is one way to rein in expenses.

2) A few other organizations check these meal receipts to figure out how many people attended the event. While this might seem intrusive to some, there is actually some logic behind this, especially if you suspect that some employees are routinely adding people to an event who have nothing to do with the business. And, that is to make sure you are in compliance with all IRS regulations related to your accountable plan status. As you may recall, one of the requirements for reporting expenses to the IRS is that the name and business relationship be listed for every attendee at an event (including meals the company pays for).

3) Then there is the latest scam being used by a very few employees to bilk their organization for money they are not entitled to. Here's how it goes. An employee takes someone out to a business lunch. They fully report the event, meeting IRS documentation requirements. However, before they pay the bill at the restaurant, they have the restaurant include a gift card intended for personal use – not as a gift to a vendor or customer. It is unlikely this can be determined from the receipt – unless the itemized receipt is requested. Requiring the itemized receipt will serve as a deterrent. Hopefully none of your employees would be foolish enough to commit this fraud and then turn in the receipt showing the gift card. So, if you move to this

requirement, do not expect to see gift cards showing up on the receipts.

Monitoring These Receipts

Now if you are thinking "uggh, more tedious work for the department" fear not. While you might require these receipts and the organization's employees might believe they are all being checked, you should not devote too much time to that task. If your policy makes managers responsible for the T&E expense reimbursement reports they approve and really does hold them accountable if they don't, you will not have much additional work. Spot check these receipts. This means looking at maybe five to ten percent of these receipts and perhaps looking at the receipts of those employees known to take liberty with their entertainment budgets.

The IRS recently conducted a number of audits with the states purpose of gathering data. Expense reimbursements are one of the three areas under scrutiny. We can only guess that they are doing this because they think there is potential additional tax revenue for the government in this area. And, there is a good reason to believe that they think some employees and/or organizations are playing games that are potentially contributing to the tax gap. Whatever the true reason, the audits should serve as a warning to those not fully documenting their expense reimbursements correctly that the days of lax attention to travel and entertainment reimbursement practices are fast coming to an end. If we are not monitoring everything we should, we need to get started.

In case it is not clear, let me state that at least at this point, getting the detailed meal receipts is not an IRS requirement. That does not mean that you should not do so, if you suspect you have any of the issues discussed above.

The Detailed Meal Receipt: How They Help Run a Tighter Reimbursement Function

Companies everywhere are starting to look at receipts in a

whole new way—and the change is not exactly what you might expect. This new approach is based on experiences organizations have had as they've reviewed documentation provided by traveling employees. Advances in technology have provided greater visibility into reimbursement requests and not everyone is pleased with what they've uncovered. Let's briefly review the history of receipts and then a look at where we're going in this arena and why.

A Little Background

The IRS requires receipts for any reimbursement in excess of $75. This legislation went into effect in 1995. As you probably realize, few companies followed suit. For a long time, $25 was the norm for the majority of organizations reimbursing employees for expenses incurred during business travel or entertainment.

What is noteworthy is how few organizations followed the IRS lead in requiring receipts for expenditures over $75, even 20+ years later.

Who Requires What

Accounts Payable Now & Tomorrow polled readers to find out if many organizations were moving up to the IRS level; after all, it's been quite some time since the $75 requirement went into effect. The data below reveals what its readers are doing when it comes to receipts for travel and entertainment by its employees.

Receipt Requirements: What Companies Require

- We require all receipts (not necessarily meal receipts)
58.90%

- We have different receipt requirement for meals?
30.06%

- We are considering requiring a detailed receipt for meals showing exactly what was ordered   26.54%

As you can see, the majority of companies now require all

receipts, although not necessarily the detailed meal receipt. That being said, slightly over one-quarter are considering adding the requirement of the detailed meal receipt.

What the Detailed Meal Receipt Can Show

So, why request a detailed meal receipt? What does it show? The following are some of the issues that can be documented through the detailed meal receipt.

- If liquor was ordered (important for those on grants)
- How many people attended (i.e. two or four, based on the number of main dishes ordered)
- Who attended – were they any kiddie meals.
- When the event took place (Friday and Saturday night meals problematic.)
- Was the meal appropriate (i.e. 12 beers and a plate of wings)
- Was a restaurant gift cards added to the bill (a new problem)

Requiring Doesn't Mean Checking Them All

Sometimes when this issue is raised, the professionals involved in the checking have an –are-you-for-real reaction because they already have too much work and not enough time in which to do it. Let's be clear. We still advocate spot checking, rather than individual verification of each receipt. Spot checking means verifying:

- 5-10% of reports, randomly selected

- All reports of known abusers

- C-level execs (if requested, by management)

- All high high-dollar expense reports.

Of course each company's definition of a high-dollar expense report is different. For some it will be all reports over $10,000 and other all reports over $2500.

The $24.95 Problem

You may be wondering why companies are moving away from the $25 receipt requirement. It seems to make a lot of sense. However more than a few are infuriated by what we call the $24.95 problem. It seems that at organizations with a $25 receipt limit, there is an unexplainably high number of requests for reimbursement in the $24 level.

This has led some to hypothesize that some employees put in for just under $25 any time they have a meal that costs anything under $25 – even if they just have a hamburger at a fast food establishment. That issue also partially explains why some organizations have a different requirement for receipts related to meals than they have for other items.

Scanning Receipts: Dealing with the Two Main Problems

When it comes to technology in accounts payable, it is sometimes a jig of two steps forward followed by one step backwards. But, we're getting there. One place where the aforementioned dance is in effect is the travel and entertainment (T&E) reimbursement function. While an automated expense reimbursement function has a lot to recommend it, there are some new issues emerging. They revolve around the scanning of receipts. But before we get to those problems and how to solve them, let's take a look at how companies are handling the scanning of T&E receipts.

How Receipts Are Handled

When AP Now surveyed readers of its weekly electronic news alert about their practices regarding receipts and scanning, it found that:

- 26% had a fully manual process with no scanning of receipts,
- 18% scanned with AP (or T&E group) getting receipts from employees and handling the scanning,
- 33% required employees to scan the receipts, and
- 23% had a variety of other practices or some combination of the above.

We asked, if employees were required to scan their own receipts, had the organization had much of a problem. Just over 18% indicated there were some issues. These problems fell into two broad categories:

- Duplicate submissions of the same receipt
- Legibility of the scans

Readers also shared their practices on how they deal with these problems.

Guarding Against Duplicate Submissions

Dealing with scans is a new skill for some employees and some apparently are submitting the same receipt more than one time. Whether this is being done through ignorance of how to use the technology or with the hopes of tricking the company into paying more than it should is irrelevant. We need to be able to identify these situations. Here are several solutions used by our readers.

1. We have a report that can be run to identify duplicate transactions.
2. At first we had issues with them scanning and then rescanning and accidentally replacing but it was just a training issue. We have been doing it now for two and a half years and do not have any issues with receipts
3. We have developed a process to check transactions on incoming expense reports against transaction history for each employee to catch duplicate expense submissions before they're paid.
4. We are using a software for T&E expenses. It was better when we had to process manually, as there was more control over what was reimbursed.
5. We had also had an issue with an individual submitting the same receipt multiple times. We have several field employees who scan in their receipts for processing, but they are required to submit the originals for the file once they return to the office before reimbursement.

When Scans Are Difficult to Read

It would be great is receipts were standardized and all were printed in at least a font size of 10. But, as those reading this are aware, that is anything but the case. Some are on tiny slips of paper, others printed with a cartridge or ribbon that should have been replaced eons ago. There's nothing we can do about those issues, but our readers have come up with some solutions for dealing with the less-than-desirable receipt. Here are their suggestions.

1) Because originals can be tiny, we allow employees to scan five or six on one page. Then this document is attached to the corresponding line items in the system. This helps alleviate the struggle some have of scanning small receipts.

2) We require employees to scan the required receipts in the same order as the expenses appear in the expense reporting tool using a Color PDF format. After scanning the receipts, we require them to open the scanned images folder on their PC and review the saved receipt images to assure that all receipts are legible and in the correct order. If all receipts are legible and in the correct order, then an only then can they attach them to their expense report.

3) The scanned images are many times cut off or blurry so they are illegible. We try to follow up with them to rescan if they still have the receipt.

4) We ask that they still attach the receipts to a page of paper in the same order they show up on the report before scanning them.

5) Because the IRS now accepts photographs of receipts, many employees take pictures with their smartphones, however, the pictures sometimes are not clear, or they don't capture the entire receipt.

6) If the receipts are illegible we require manager approval or the original before payment

7) One problem with faxing is quality fax machine and

resolution used. We recommend scanning and attaching a PDF and instruct employees who fax to use a good quality fax machine with the resolution set on 'Fine'

8) Sometime receipts aren't legible after scanning / faxing which is why we request they keep the originals for 90 days. Generally, our audits are completed within that time frame

We definitely advocate the use of technology in accounts payable and the scanning of receipts falls under that heading. But, we also advocate studying the outcomes of the use of technology to identify any new concerns and work to create solutions that fix that problem. As you can see, that is exactly what respondents to the AP Now survey did with their receipts issue.

Concluding Thoughts

Detailed meal receipts reveal a lot of information related to business entertainment. What's more, the simple act of requiring the receipt may deter for some employees considering playing games with their expense reports as they know they can't mask their games in the totals. If you suspect there are issues with travel that you can't identify from the credit card receipts being submitted, consider asking for the detailed meal receipt.

Finally, keep in mind that just because you require the receipts doesn't mean you have to check them all. Of course, if your travel reimbursement process is automated, then checking 100% of receipts is not a problem.

Chapter 6

Emerging Payment Frauds, both Large and Small

Businesses aren't the only ones who use technology to hone their skills and become more efficient. Unfortunately, smart crooks are doing the same thing. They study the banking system and find new weaknesses and innovations they can take advantage of. Thus we've had some new frauds on the landscape over the last few years – and we expect there will be some new ones in the coming years. This, it is imperative that professionals who operate in the business world stay on top of new frauds. But alas, not all fraud starts on the outside. While most employees are honest, a few can't resist playing games with their expense reimbursement requests and so we've included some advice on that issue as well. In this chapter we examine:

- Travel & Entertainment Reimbursement Shenanigans
- How to Protect Your Organization against ACH Fraud
- ACH Fraud Case Study
- Cyber-Payment Fraud: Innovative Swindles and Best-Practice Protection Tips
- Changing Best Practices to Fight Fraud

Before we get to the electronic payment frauds, we take a look at a few ways some employees are finding to pad their expense reports.

Travel & Entertainment Reimbursement Shenanigans

We use the word shenanigans to differentiate between large dollar fraud and smaller dollar fraud, typically committed by playing games with a process. But just because the dollars are not as big as some of the other frauds does not mean this is an issue you shouldn't take seriously. Fraud is fraud whether there's a dollar or a million dollars involved. What's more, typically small frauds, if undetected, will grow larger with time and the cumulative damage to your bottom line can be significant.

Why Shenanigans Matters

Sometimes people wonder why we think small frauds are so important. There are several reasons. For starters, in more than a few instances, when an organization starts investigating a small fraud, they uncover a larger fraud going on elsewhere in the organization. It seems that the crook cannot resist the temptation of trying to get his or her hands on a few more dollars.

Then there is the issue of the company's accountable plan status with the IRS. This is the Holy Grail when it comes to taxes. You may unintentionally endanger that status if you are reimbursing employees for items that are clearly fraudulent.

As mentioned above, frauds tend to grow. Thieves are never satisfied and will continually up the ante, trying to get a little more each time. So, what started as a small petty fraud may evolve into something much larger, over time, if undetected.

Morale within the organization may also suffer, if it is generally known that an employee is playing games and management is ignoring the issue. What's more other employees may feel embolden to emulate the thieves' successes.

And finally, if you are a public company there is the issue of compliance with the Sarbanes-Oxley Act. Allowing an employee to put in for reimbursement for items that are clearly not covered by the policy is a sign of weak internal controls.

Common Methodologies Used

Employees use a number of techniques to flitch funds they are not entitled to. They may:

- Mischaracterize expenses, i.e. put in for a personal meal as a business expense;

- Request multiple reimbursements for the same item, either putting in for the expense in more than one month or using two different payment vehicles (such as expense reimbursement and petty cash);

- Overstate expenses such as claiming a bigger tip than the one that was given;

- Invent expenses such as claiming a tip when none was given.

Execution of Common Shenanigans

Employees can be quite creative when it comes to extorting cash from their employer through the expense reimbursement process. Here's a few of the approaches they use:

1) Claiming more than was actually spent. Anytime a cash payment is made there is the opportunity to claim reimbursement for a higher amount. This can be tips to the cleaning staff in a hotel when none were left or if a taxi ride was taken the amount of the ride and tip can be increased. There are a myriad of other games to play when cash is used. It is one of the reasons companies should strongly discourage the use of cash.

2) Changing the tip on a meal receipt is an easy task, if a corporate card is not required. By giving a low tip and having that run through on their personal credit card, the thieving employee then takes the second receipt and adds a more appropriate tip. The receipt with the more appropriate tip is used on the expense report.

3) Putting in for more mileage than was actually driven. This is getting easier to catch thanks to online sites giving

directions, which can be used to estimate mileage. Additionally, some of the newer third-party T&E software will flag mileage that seems inappropriate.

4) Double dipping can be accomplished in several ways. Either two employees who shared a meal or cab ride can both put in for the total expense or one employee can put in for reimbursement of the same expense on two different reports or use two different reimbursement methodologies i.e. petty cash and expense reporting.

5) Out and out altering receipts is another method unscrupulous employees use to get reimbursement for more than they are owed. This may or may not be obvious depending on the skill level of the employee in question.

The Gift Card Issue

As you may have noticed, many restaurants offer gift cards. A few go so far as to add a line to the credit card receipt so the diner can add on a gift card at the time he or she is adding the tip to the bill. This is fine if the person is paying for the meal themselves.

Unfortunately, a few unscrupulous employees have taken to adding on a gift card when taking a business associate out for a meal. If they gave the gift card to the associate this might be acceptable. However, they are pocketing the gift card for personal use. This is just one of the reasons a growing number of organizations are now requiring the detailed meal receipt. We'll discuss that a little further in this chapter.

The Common Solution

You have probably figured out that there's one easy way to get rid of a lot of the problems discussed. Have a corporate credit card and require it be used for all purchases. Do not give employees the option of using it. Those who want to play games will most definitely decide not to use the card, if given the choice. While this won't address all the issues, it will put a serious dent in the problem.

The Solution: The Detailed Meal Receipt

Companies everywhere are starting to look at receipts in a whole new way—and the change is not exactly what you might expect. This new approach is based on experiences organizations have had as they've reviewed documentation provided by traveling employees. Advances in technology have provided greater visibility into reimbursement requests and not everyone is pleased with what they've uncovered. Let's briefly review the history of receipts and then a look at where we're going in this arena and why.

A Little Background

The IRS requires receipts for any reimbursement in excess of $75. This legislation went into effect in 1995. As you probably realize, few companies followed suit. For a long time, $25 was the norm for the majority of organizations reimbursing employees for expenses incurred during business travel or entertainment.

What is noteworthy is how few organizations followed the IRS lead in requiring receipts for expenditures over $75, even almost 20 years later.

What the Detailed Meal Receipt Can Show

So, why request a detailed meal receipt? What does it show? The following are some of the issues that can be documented through the detailed meal receipt.

- If liquor was ordered (important for those on grants)
- How many people attended (i.e. two or four, based on the number of main dishes ordered)
- Who attended – were they any kiddie meals.
- When the event took place (Friday and Saturday night meals problematic.)
- Was the meal appropriate (i.e. 12 beers and a plate of wings)
- Was a restaurant gift cards added to the bill (a new problem)

As discussed in the previous chapter, requiring all receipts doesn't mean checking them all.

Concluding Thoughts

Detailed meal receipts reveal a lot of information related to business entertainment. What's more, the simple act of requiring the receipt may deter for some employees considering playing games with their expense reports as they know they can't mask their games in the totals. If you suspect there are issues with travel that you can't identify from the credit card receipts being submitted, consider asking for the detailed meal receipt.

Finally, keep in mind that just because you require the receipts doesn't mean you have to check them all. Of course, if your travel reimbursement process is automated, then checking 100% of receipts is not a problem.

How to Protect Your Organization against ACH Fraud

ACH fraud, sometimes referred to as electronic payment fraud, is a threat every organization must deal with on a daily basis. For no organization is exempt from the prying grasps of fraudsters trying to get into any bank account they can. Making this issue even more serious than many readers might be aware is the fact that some of these thefts are being masterminded by organized crime located in other countries.

Myths that Cause Problems

Fraud in the ACH world can do serious damage. Unfortunately, many organizations don't take it seriously until it's too late. They believe one of the following – all of which are FALSE:

1. We use positive pay for checks and it will protect us
2. We don't make electronic payments so we are not at risk
3. We're too big no one would dare try to steal from us
4. We're too small for anyone to be interested in us
5. Our bank will eat any losses for payments we don't authorize

Unfortunately, all of these beliefs cause trouble. If you are using positive pay with your checks, you are protected against check fraud, that's all. It does nothing to protect against ACH fraud.

Not making electronic payments means you don't make electronic payments from your own account. If you don't take the proper precautions, someone else will. So, please, don't rely on non-participation as an excuse to do nothing.

Size, also is no guarantee. Crooks will steal wherever they can. Being too small or too big offers absolutely no protection.

And finally, banks cannot afford to eat losses nor are they responsible for them legally. Do not be lulled into a false sense of security thinking that your organization is not a target. Neither non-participation in the market nor size of your organization will safeguard your accounts. Only you can do that by taking the necessary steps as discussed further in this chapter. But before we get to the strategies you can use, we have a quick review of the growth of this type of fraud and a very brief description of the types of ACH fraud now being perpetrated against organizations just like yours.

Electronic Payment Fraud

Without a doubt, crooks have turned to the ACH to perpetrate some sophisticated frauds. These crimes are growing and no one is immune. The crooks involved are increasingly sophisticated and the funds they steal often unrecoverable. It is important that everyone involved with payments understand the time constraints associated with identifying fraudulent ACH transactions.

As consumers, readers have 60 days to notify their financial institutions of unauthorized ACH transactions in their personal accounts. These include both ACH debits against their accounts and unauthorized ACH credits initiated from their accounts. As indicated earlier, the crooks in this arena are very smart. However, and this is a big one, anyone other than a consumer has <u>only</u> 24 hours to notify their bank of an unauthorized transaction.

There is no way around this. Monthly bank reconciliations won't cut it. Identifying a fraudulent transaction 30 days after the fact is too late. The money is gone. Therefore, we recommend daily account reconciliations. We also recommend using certain bank fraud prevention products, discussed in detail further on in this chapter.

Growth in ACH Fraud

If you go back five or more years you won't even find ACH fraud listed in any of the fraud surveys. However, that is changing and unfortunately changing quickly. Not only is fraud now included but the number of different types of ACH fraud is growing.

Thieves involved in this type of fraud are usually very smart and technologically sophisticated. They also (unfortunately) have a very good understanding of how the banking system works. They use this knowledge, along with their computer hacking skills to create new ways of getting their hands on your organization's money.

The evolution in this arena has occurred at lightning speed and is truly frightening. Just as the banking and business community develop practices and products to thwart their latest fraud, the crooks come up with another "innovation."

Types of ACH Fraud

The evolution of ACH fraud has been quite rapid. Just a few short years ago, the banking community was primarily concerned about the first type of fraud. Now, that has expanded. ACH fraud can be broken into give general types, although there is not guarantee that in the future we won't have a sixth and seventh and possibly more. They are as follows:

1) Representing positive pay rejects as ACH debits (unauthorized ACH debits)

2) Account hijacking also called corporate account takeover (typically via the initiation of ACH credits)

3) Reverse phishing – redirecting of electronic payments from a legitimate vendor to the fraudster

4) e-Check payments to a third party using your bank account information

5) Falsified e-mails coming from legitimate organizations containing either an attachment or a link to an illicit website. This is an alternate approach to getting information needed for an account hijacking.

There will be others as the crooks in this arena are very smart. They understand how the technology works, how the banking system operates and take advantage of this knowledge for their own benefit—at your expense.

Prevention

While you can't stop someone from trying to steal from your organization, you can make it so difficult they are not successful. What follows is a list of tactics any organization can use to prevent a fraudster from winning when trying to steal from your firm using the ACH.

1) Set up a separate computer for online banking activity only. More on this below.

2) Put ACH blocks on all accounts where ACH activity is not to be initiated; if you are paying using ACH credits, put ACH debit blocks on your accounts.

3) Put ACH filters on accounts where ACH debit activity is permitted.

4) Set up a single account for incoming wire transfers, allowing no other activity in that account. Sweep it each night into another account.

5) Do not give wire transfer information over the phone.

6) Issue refund checks from a separate account with a low-

dollar limit.

7) Regular update of security and anti-virus software.

The Separate Computer Strategy

The FBI has issued a press release warning businesses, municipal governments, and school districts that they are the primary targets of the newest type of electronic payment fraud. These crooks are stealing the online credentials of legitimate organizations and then using this information to steal hundreds of thousands of dollars from them. What's even worse is when the fraud unravels, unwitting individuals are left holding the bag – and these people rarely have the money to repay the stolen funds.

This separate PC should be used for online banking transactions and online banking transactions only, no exceptions. It should not be used for surfing the web or email, as that is how key-capturing malware is sometimes surreptitiously downloaded onto the computer, providing the fraudsters with the information they need to take over an account.

Companies should also resist the temptation to let a temp use that computer. One of the easiest ways to do this is to NOT put a copy of Office (Word, Excel, PowerPoint and Access) on the machine. Also, make sure whoever uses the computer for the online banking activity, logs off as soon as they are finished. This helps remove the temptation to use the computer for a quick Internet search.

Detection

Sometimes, no matter how hard you try, an unauthorized transaction gets through. If that happens, all is not lost. If you notify the bank within 24 hours, they can retrieve your money. The following strategies are recommended for detecting unauthorized activity.

1) Perform daily bank reconciliations to identify unauthorized activity.

2) Notify the bank immediately of unauthorized activity.

Readers should note that even if they detect a fraud outside the afore-mentioned 24 hour time period, they should still contact their bank. The bank may still be able to recover some or all of the missing funds.

ACH Fraud Protection: Bank Products

Electronic payment fraud is nasty, unsettling and expensive. What's more, every organization is a potential target, regardless of whether they make electronic payments or not. Some think, "oh, we don't participate in that arena so we're safe." That is categorically not true. What's more, organizations who are hit with an unauthorized debit have only 24 hours to alert their banks. Otherwise, they have no recourse. As the sophisticated crooks involved in electronic payment fraud crank into high gear, it is more important than ever that every professional take the appropriate steps to protect their organization. The banks can help as well. This is a look at what's currently available from the banking community.

Background

Before we discuss the products available now and as well as those introduced in the coming years, it is important that readers understand they need to read the product descriptions very closely. Unfortunately, it is not like positive pay where we can say one name and everyone knows what the product does.

Read the product description and make sure it does what you think it does. Also, make sure you understand what, if any, your obligations are regarding the use of the bank product.

Bank Products

There are four types of products either available or very close to being available. They are:

1) ACH Blocks. These are instructions given a bank to block ACH activity. You can either have all ACH activity blocked or just ACH debit activity. This needs to be done

on an account by account basis. What many organizations do if they want or need to allow ACH debits is to limit that activity to one or two accounts. They then put ACH blocks on all the other accounts. If you do not want to allow any ACH debit activity, put an ACH debit block on the account.

2) ACH Filters. Should you allow ACH debits on one or more accounts, you can put a filter in place. This is a list of organizations that you have given permission to debit your account. The bank won't check the dollar amount, just the entity debiting your account. If they initiate an unauthorized transaction, the filter won't catch it. But, the filter is a big step in the right direction.

The first two products are currently available and most financial institutions offer them. The next two products are just starting to find their way into the marketplace. If your bank hasn't offered them to you, call them and ask about it.

3) ACH Payee File. This is similar to the ACH filter, but works when you initiate the payment. With this product, you supply the bank with a list of entities and people you intend to pay using ACH. Then when your list of payments comes through, if there is a payment to an entity not on your preauthorized list, the payment will not be made. This product helps protect your organization against losses from an account takeover.

4) Notification of ACH Debits. With this product, any time an ACH debit hits your account, the bank notifies you and asks if it should honor the transaction. Now, if this seems like a lot of work, consider this. Most organizations only allow a few entities to initiate ACH debits against their account. Hence, the number of phone calls should be small – unless a crook is trying to debit your account and you want those calls.

Whether we like it or not, ACH fraud continues to grow. What's more the crooks who focus on it are very sophisticated and they are continually devising new ways to steal from organizations just like yours. Thus, the protections that work today, may not address the problems that emerge next week or next year. So, it is imperative that once you create the perfect protection plan, you don't rest on your laurels. Continue to monitor the fraud situation. And of course, continue to talk to your bank about new products it develops to help protect your organization from this insidious crime.

ACH Fraud Case Study: It Could Happen to Any Organization—including Yours

A recent cyber-theft utilizing ACH demonstrates how important it is for all organizations to take proper security precautions. The victim was a medium-sized not-for-profit, a typical target for this type of fraud. What's more the events also show a shift in attitudes over the responsibility issue. There are some lessons to be learned for every company. Let's take a look at what happened.

The Theft

The Metropolitan Entertainment & Convention Authority, a nonprofit organization in Omaha Nebraska was hit with fraudulent ACH transactions totaling $217,000. It is believed that an employee at the organization fell for a phishing e-mail that downloaded malware software onto his computer. The employee opened an email attachment infected with a virus that stole the information. Through this software the technologically-savvy thieves were able to obtain the login and password credentials.

The cyber-crooks then added their own "hires" to the payroll. The payments went to the money mules hired through work-at-home scams. The heist was, like many others, based in an Eastern European country. Luckily, it was uncovered early and all but $70,000 was recovered.

Reaction

The organization took responsibility for the attack, surprising many in the financial community. The reason for this is illuminating. Their bank had offered several security options which the Convention Authority had passed on.

The explanation offered was that they thought the security recommendations made by the bank would be "administratively burdensome." Like many organizations they did not believe they would be victimized. The organization stepped up to the plate and did not expect its bank to compensate it for its losses.

Lessons Learned

For starters, it is imperative that every organization realize it could be a target. These thieves are known to focus their attentions on small and mid-sized businesses that are less likely to employ best fraud prevention practices. Many are unaware and others think it would never happen to them. While there have been instances of large companies being hit by ACH fraud, it is not believed that it happens often. These organizations take the proper precautions to protect themselves. Typically, their bankers also make them aware of the latest frauds. Although it does not appear to be a factor in this theft, many of these cyber-heists occur at times when offices are known to be lightly staffed. This includes the week between Christmas and New Year's day, late August etc.

Once this realization has sunk in that your organization could be a target, talk to your bankers. Ask what products they offer to protect against this insidious type of fraud. Pay close attention to the explanation of what the products actually do. There has not been much in the way of uniform protections so it is imperative that you understand what each actually does. Also ask what else they suggest. They will probably suggest, among other things, that you set up a separate computer for all your online banking activity.

This particular situation reinforces that recommendation. Your online banking should be handled on a separate computer used for NOTHING else. Few organizations follow this advice despite the fact that it is relatively inexpensive to implement. A stand-alone computer costs less than $1,000 – and if used only for online banking needs little other software. In fact, not installing other software on it will reduce the chances that someone will be tempted to use it in case of an emergency. By the way, this recommendation comes not only from those involved in the financial community but from the FBI as well.

And finally, realize that fraud is continually evolving with crooks finding new and devious ways to practice their trade. As quickly as the financial community finds ways to protect itself against the latest wave of payment fraud, the crooks find a new way to illicitly get your organization's money. This means it is imperative that every organization keep abreast of all the new types of frauds as well as the protections available to protect their funds. It also means continually revising processes to address the latest concerns. The creation of new types of electronic payment frauds, unfortunately, is an ongoing process, not one that is likely to remain static.

Concluding Thoughts

This is a particularly insidious type of fraud and every organization is a potential target. Not only is it important that you update your procedures and protections now, but it is critical you keep on top of this issue as crooks are continually identifying new ways to get at your account.

Cyber-Payment Fraud: Innovative Swindles and Best-Practice Protection Tips

It should probably come as no surprise to anyone involved in the financial world to learn that crooks are adding technology to their arsenal of tools used to defraud anyone they can.

Unsurprisingly, they've ratcheted their game up a notch by turning their attention to corporate bank accounts – where the payoff can be much bigger than robbing the average Joe or Jane.

The individuals involved in cyber-payment fraud targeting employees acting on behalf of their employers are smart, understand banking and the Internet much better than most, and do their homework. When they act, for the most part, it is with great care and precision. AP Now believes that understanding how the frauds are perpetrated is the first step in protecting against the crime. This piece focuses on the frauds and contains some best-practice prevention and detection advice at the end.

The Frauds

Before explaining the newer frauds, it is imperative that every reader understands this is not a static environment. The individuals involved in this type of thievery are continually finding new ways to defraud anyone they can. It is imperative you keep current on this issue. Here are some of the more common newer frauds:

- *Account Masquerading*. This involves the takeover of C-level executives email account. The account may actually be taken over or the e-mail address spoofed. The perpetrator then uses the account to direct a lower level employee to either send money or divulge confidential information to a third party ASAP. Often, by the time the fraud unravels, the money or information is gone. Recourse is difficult because an employee of the organization initiated the transaction.

- *Account Hijacking*. This fraud involved the malicious takeover of a company's bank account. Once in control the crook creates and sends to the bank an ACH file with funds going to parties controlled by the crook. Since the crook has accessed the proper protocols (passwords etc.) the bank has no way of recognizing this file did not come from the company.

- *Reverse Phishing.* This is a variation of an old fraud. It involves sending a carefully spoofed e-mail to the appropriate person in accounts payable pretending to be from one of the company's customers. The e-mail explains the supplier has closed an old bank account and requests that future payments be made to a new account and the bank account number is provided. The crooks involved are very good at incorporating logos and other material in the e-mail to make it look legitimate. There have been reports of savvy crooks mixing this one up and sending a letter through the post with change of bank account information; so be suspicious of everything.

- *The e-mail-in-the-middle Scam.* In this fraud, the crook manages to insert himself in the middle of an e-mail conversation between a supplier and a customer. The fraud can play either party. It either directs the purchasing company to send payments to a new bank account because of a purported audit or directs the supplier to ship goods to a location controlled by the crook. Typically these transactions are rush transactions for whatever reason the crook can concoct. There have also been instances of this type of fraud involving payments that have to be made before a ship can be unloaded.

5 Simple Steps Every Company Should Take

Clearly, every organization needs to update its fraud protection arsenal of practices. What follows is a look at five new ones that should be used by every organization concerned about fraud. These practices include:

1. Set up a separate computer to be used for online banking and nothing else. This means no surfing the Internet or checking email on this computer. This will help prevent an account takeover.

2. Institute a process to verify any change in business practice (be it ordering, delivery or bank account change) using contact information already on hand.

3. Upgrade master vendor file protocols to include contact information. This is not something that is considered high priority in many organizations. It is not enough to just collect the data when you begin a business relationship. Regularly update the contact information so it will be accurate when needed.

4. Use the forward key instead of the reply key when responding to e-mails. The e-mail software will autofill the address. This will prevent someone from inadvertently responding to a spoofed e-mail. The response will go to the individual the fraudster was trying to impersonate and the fraud will fall apart. On the face of it, this sounds easy enough to do. But, to actually remember to hit the forward key is not as simple as it might first appear.

5. Begin doing daily bank reconciliations instead of monthly ones. This will enable you to identify any unauthorized transactions and notify the bank quickly. Time is of the essence when it comes to recovering unauthorized transactions. Wait more than 24 hours and the bank may not be able to recover your funds. Since bank reconciliations have to be done anyway, why not start sooner.

Changing Best Practices in AP to Fight Fraud and Tighten Controls

The new practices discussed below are the ones focus on changes now in use to instill tighter controls and fight fraud. They all involve process changes rather than an expenditure for software or hardware. You may already have integrated some or all of these practices into your operation.

Practice #1: Keeping up now means keeping up with new frauds and new fraud prevention techniques. Unfortunately, it's not only businesses taking advantage of new technology to improve their processes, crooks are as well. What is truly regrettable is the understanding these fraudsters have of the banking system and the ingenuity they have used to devise new frauds.

Practice #2: Job rotation is not something we normally thought about in accounts payable. But, if you have more than two or three processors, consider moving them around rather than leaving them handling the same vendors for years on end. Yes, the benefit of that approach is they get to know the account really well. This can be beneficial in resolving problems or if you have to ask for a special favor. However, and this is a biggie, it also means they may get so friendly, a few will concoct a plan to defraud one or both organizations. While this won't happen often, it has occurred frequently enough for fraud experts to recommend this course of action.

Practice #3: Likewise, mandatory vacations help protect an organization against an ongoing employee fraud. The theory beyond this recommendation is that if an employee is perpetrating an ongoing fraud, it will unravel if they are forced to be away from the office for five (or more) consecutive days. For this tactic to be effective, it is imperative that someone other than the employee perform their job during this period. The strategy falls apart if the employee simply performs his or her job from home.

Practice #4: Rather than have employees handling online banking using their own computers for this task, designate a single PC for online banking activities. This computer should be used for NOTHING else, especially e-mail or surfing the Internet. This tactic protects the organization against a corporate account takeover by savvy fraudsters who utilize the

Internet to perpetrate their crimes. While this does not happen often, the damage it inflicts when it does occur is massive and every organization, regardless of size, is advised to protect against it. The cost of a computer is small so there is no financial reason for ignoring this piece of advice.

Practice #5: When responding to an e-mail, especially if it has anything to do with finances (like changes to bank account information), hit the forward key instead of the reply key to respond to confirm. When you hit the forward key, you will have to type in the e-mail address of the person you are responding to. If it is someone you regularly do business with, the address should auto-fill. When the message is sent, if the party you thought had sent the original note did not, he or she will respond accordingly – and you will not have honored a request from a crook. Spoofing of e-mail addresses is just one more way fraudsters attempt to get their hands on your organization's funds.

Practice #6: Close off system access for employees who have either been promoted or who have left the company. This step is often overlooked and leaves the organization wide open to segregation of duties issues. By closing off the access as part of the organization's standard separation and promotion practices, this threat is eliminated. Some groups neglect to do this for departing employees forgetting that a few of them may be hired back at a future date.

Practice #7: Check the US Department of Treasury's Office of Foreign Assets Control (OFAC) as well as its Specially Designated Nationals List (SDN) lists at least monthly to ensure payments are not going to parties on the SDN list. The reality is you are supposed to check payments against this list before you make each payment, but few other than the credit card companies actually do this. Some make it a part of the new vendor set-up to check against the list. This is a good first step. If you simply can't incorporate the practice of checking before each payment, try and do it at least once a month. At least this will demonstrate a good-faith effort on your part to conform with the law, should you inadvertently make a payment you shouldn't. In Canada, check against the Office of the Superintendent of Financial Institutions (OSFI) list.

Practice #8: Provide some Foreign Corrupt Practices Act (FCPA) training for the accounts payable staff. As several recent high-profile cases demonstrate, the Department of Justice is serious about enforcing the anti-bribery legislation currently on the books. By providing the accounts payable staff, the last set of eyes to see a payment before it goes out the door, with some training on what to look for, the organization can show good faith, if it inadvertently makes a bribe.

Practice #9: Regularly update contact information in the master vendor file in order to help protect the organization against fraud. This way, when a questionable transaction shows up, you can contact the legitimate vendor to get clarification. If you haven't ever collected contact information or haven't updated it, this task will become infinitely more difficult.

Practice #10: A growing number of organizations are now requiring the detailed meal receipt for restaurant expenditures. The reason for this is simple. Too many employees play games with their expense reimbursement requests and companies have had enough. What's more, the detailed meal receipt helps those with grants that include special requirements related to reimbursable meals.

Concluding Thoughts

Some of the advice offered in this chapter comes from the FBI and the FDIC. Both groups were so concerned about the level and intensity of the cyber-crimes, they've issued advice several times over the last few years. This is in sharp contrast to the past when they refrained from commenting on fraud.

None of the recommended practices cost much, if anything, to implement. However, they do require a change in routine as well as a change in thinking. Staffers, at all levels, should be encouraged to question anything that looks the least bit out of the ordinary. At one organization, a masquerading fraud was uncovered simply because the employee who received the purported instructions said "it didn't sound the way her CEO usually wrote" so she investigated.

While we wish this were the end of all new types of cyber-frauds, that is not likely to be the case. So, in closing we'd like to remind readers to be alert for new types of fraud. We're not sure what they will look like, but we're pretty certain we haven't seen the last new cyber-fraud.

Chapter 7
Vendor Portals in Accounts Payable

There's been a lot of discussion about portals in accounts payable in the last few years. That conversation has gotten louder in recent months and with good reason. Vendor portals (occasionally referred to as supplier portals) are just another step on the path to automation that is currently going on in accounts payable. But all portals are not the same. Let's take a look at some of the differences.

- What You Need to Know to Get Started
- How Vendor Portals Can Help the ACH Change of Bank Account Problem
- How Vendor Portals Help You Address The Contact Information Issue
- The Future of Vendor Portals

What Is a Vendor Portal?

Before we get started, let's start with a basic definition so we all are on the same page. A portal is an interactive, online repository of information that allows access to a variety of self-service applications. There are many kinds of portals and accounts payable isn't the only function taking advantage of them. Any time you sign up for free publications and then selected the different news alerts you'd like to receive you are using a type of portal.

In the accounts payable arena vendor portals are all the rage. It is important to understand that unlike the publishing world where anyone can sign up, vendor portals are by invitation only. It is not the kind of 'Open House' where anyone who finds your website can sign up. Your vendors should not be able to sign up unless you've sent them a link. Otherwise you'll end up with crooks signing themselves up to be your suppliers.

What Do Portals Do?

Portals basically collect information and allow self-service for many tasks that would normally require an interaction between the vendor and the customer. The most common example of a portal that replaces communication is the ones that allow vendors to sign into the portal and check on the payment status of open invoices. This keeps the where's-my-money calls out of accounts payable.

These can be stand-alone portals or part of a larger enterprise. Some readers may remember the development roughly a decade ago of interactive voice recognition (IVR) systems that allowed vendors to get this information over the phone. The IVRs were similar to the services offered by many pharmacies that allow you to call in and key in your prescription numbers for refills.

There are many different portals that can be used in accounts payable. For example, probably the most common portals are those used in connection with the electronic delivery of invoices either by a third party or directly by the vendors. In the case of a third party, it 'collects' invoices from a number of vendors and delivers them electronically to the customer. Alternatively, a number of companies have set up portals allowing their vendors to deliver the invoices online by signing into the portal and uploading the documents or information. It should be noted that this is different than the simple emailing of invoices to an individual.

What Do Vendor Portals Do in AP?

To be clear, not everyone means the same thing when they talk about a vendor portal. Portals in use today in accounts payable cover a wide range. They can be very simple handling only one or two tasks to the more complex. Here are some examples of tasks handled in portals.

1) Delivery of invoices
2) Status of invoices
3) Status of payments
4) Automatic escalations of invoice approvals
5) Dispute resolution
6) Other vendor inquiries
7) Vendor setup for the master vendor file
8) Updates of information in the master vendor file
9) Track vendor diversity for government reporting
10) Track W-9 collection
11) Track W-9 verification using IRS TIN Matching

If at first glance this looks like it will replace most of the accounts payable department, we've overstated the case. What it will do is to remove a lot of the manual and clerical work handled in many accounts payable departments. But, these portals have to be used intelligently.

Let's take a look at the vendor setting itself up in the master vendor file. While the vendor can input its own information, care needs to be taken. If you just let vendors input their information directly, few will adhere to the rigid coding standard best-practice accounts payable functions insist on using. It's pointless to even try and get them to do that. What this means is after the vendor puts in its information; someone will have to review the information and change it, where appropriate, to conform to your coding standards.

So, while on some fronts portals definitely reduce work in accounts payable, they will create some new positions requiring a different set of skills. Portals are here and their benefits clear cut. It is imperative that organizations figure out what role they will play in the accounts payable function.

How Do We Get One?

There are two basic ways organizations get portals. They either purchase them or build them. Which approach your organization takes will depend on what the organization wants to do with it and how much customization will be required. If the organization has many unique requirements, the build-it-yourself approach might be called for. Alternatively, a third party model can be purchased and customized. That can get costly.

The approach most organizations are taking is to buy a pre-built model and if necessary, customize. Some of the models available are built so you can do a certain amount of customization as part of the basic price. From a cost standpoint, this is definitely a benefit. Also, a few of the models (especially the ones involved with electronic invoicing) are available on a SaaS or pay-as-you go basis.
There are a few models that shift the burden of payment from the customer to the vendor. This is not a good idea from a vendor relations standpoint. You'll occasionally hear a company bragging that their vendors don't mind paying. *Really???* Typically this only works when there is an 800-pound gorilla in the relationship.

Expect to pay for the portals but also realize that after the portal is operational, your cost savings will exceed the expense involved in setting up and utilizing the portal on an ongoing basis.

Those interested in invoicing portals can start with the e-invoicing vendors. Go to their websites and sign up for an online demo. They are happy to give them. Some schedule these demos on a regular basis. Go to as many as you have time for and ask a lot of questions. Once you've narrowed your search, it's time for some serious discussion with the vendors in question.

How Vendor Portals Can Help the ACH Change of Bank Account Problem

As you are probably painfully aware, the crooks operating in the ACH fraud arena are very smart and understand how banking processes work even better than most professionals in the field. They've figured out a nifty way to get businesses to send them money simply by sending an e-mail or two. Let's take a look at how the fraud works, what you can do to prevent it and how the new vendor portals can help.

How The Fraud Works

First the crooks study your business and figure out who is making payments. This is an imprecise "art" so they don't always get it right. But, they often do. Once they have that important piece of information, they take a look at who your top vendors are likely to be. This is usually fairly easy to do. They may not be able to identify all your vendors, but they really only need one or two.

Once they have the two pieces of information needed to perpetrate the fraud, they prepare a simple e-mail purporting to come from the vendor in question. It tells its customer (that's you) that the vendor has changed back accounts and asks that all future funds be sent to a new back account. The number is provided.

These e-mails look legitimate. They may even include the logo of the company the crook is pretending to be. This is easy enough to get off most websites. In some cases, the e-mail address itself may even have been spoofed. So, simply verifying the e-mail came from the company is not enough. Nor is calling the company using the phone number provided in the e-mail, for if the e-mail is fraudulent, the phone number will be as well.

Detecting the Fraud

So, if you can't reply to the e-mail or use the phone number provided in the e-mail, how can you verify that the request is legitimate? The reality is that at the end of the day, most of these requests will be from your vendors. However, one wrong payment can make a serious dent in your organization's bottom line.

The best practice approach is to verify the request is legitimate by contacting the vendor using information you already have on hand. While at first glance this may seem easy enough, consider this. When was the last time you updated your vendor contact information? Regularly collecting and updating this information now has to be included in the work of any best practice accounts payable organization.

Using Vendor Portals

Vendor portals can help with this issue in more ways than you might imagine. For starters, most of the products on the market today are self-service models, meaning the vendors enter in their own information. This doesn't mean you won't have to do some verification after they've entered the data but it does cut down on the work being done by the folks managing the master vendor file function. The online portals do make it easier to both collect and update vendor contact information, which is needed from time to time.

There is another way vendor portals help with this specific issue. Since the vendor is responsible for input of all information, including change of bank account information, there is no need for an e-mail alerting you to a change. The vendor simply signs into the portal and updates its banking information, if there is a change. With this approach, you never have to verify a change again. And, you don't have to worry about the change of account e-mails. You shouldn't get any legitimate ones taking this approach.

The Contact Information Problem: Are You Collecting All the Contact Information You Need?

When most people think about accounts payable issues and problems, few focus on whether they collected contact information from their vendors and if they have, whether the right contact information was amassed. And the few that do address the contract information issue rarely consider it once it's collected in the first place. However, as we dive into the new and complex accounts payable arena, this data—or rather the lack of it is becoming—an issue. In this section we examine why you might need contract information as well as a best practice approach to its collection and maintenance. But before we get to that, let's dissect the contact information issue.

The Issue

Typically when a vendor is set up in the master vendor file, there is some urgency to get the task done. This is usually because the vendor is waiting to be paid. Hence, some information is sometimes left out with the emphasis on getting the data needed to pay the vendor. This might be address information and perhaps the W-9. If an electronic payment is to be made, then banking information might also be collected.

If there is a spot for vendor contact information, this might be omitted or it might be filled out with the vendor's sales person. Rarely is a contact for AR or treasury included. And, this is the information usually needed by accounts payable. Even if AR or treasury contact information is collected, it is almost never updated.

The first crack in the contact information shell appeared when it looked like we were going to have to issue a 1099 for every payment made. Although that legislation was repealed, it demonstrated that many organizations had a problem with their contact information in the master vendor file. The only address they had in their master vendor file was the Remit-To address, which frequently is a bank lockbox. This is of little use if you need to contact the vendor.

The next crack in the vendor contact information began to emerge as ACH fraud took an even uglier than normal turn. Crooks emulating vendors started sending in 'change of bank account requests.' Without readily accessible contact information, it is difficult to verify whether the change request came from the vendor or a crook. And, it is now not only a recommended best practice, but a practical necessity, that these requests be verified with the vendor using information you already have on hand—not information provided in the e-mail request. If you never asked for the information or it is several years old, you'll have a lot of work to do before you can decide whether you should honor the request.

Why You Might Need It

There are a number of reasons you might need to contact your vendors. You might only need to get in touch with a few, in which case the tracking down of current contact information might not be too oppressive. But, if you needed to do a mass mailing, getting current contact information could be overwhelming. Here are some reasons why you might want to communicate with vendors.

- Contact vendors to change your terms or other policies;
- Contact vendors to get W-9 information;
- Contact vendors to verify change of bank account request.

A Best Practice Approach

Once organizations realize the importance of collecting and updating vendor contact information for accounts payable to use, the following three steps can be used.

- Step 1. Collect the information when the vendor is first set up.
- Step 2. Verify as much of the information from third-party sources as possible.
- Step 3. Update the information on an annual basis or whenever the vendor alerts you there is a change.

Unfortunately, few vendors realize they should notify their customers' accounts payable departments with this data.

Another useful step, especially if you allow a vendor to be set up without complete information, is to periodically run reports on the master vendor file showing vendors with missing information. The information for those vendors should be updated to make it complete.

Updating the Information

You may be moaning as you read this thinking what a massive task updating contact information will be. It doesn't have to be. For starters, if you are lucky enough to be using a vendor self-service portal for your master vendor file, you can simply send a reminder e-mail to your vendors reminding them to update their contact information.

But, assuming you are not yet utilizing such a facility. We're not going to sugar coat this. This won't be a simple task. However, this is definitely something you could hire a temp to do. With a little bit of explanation and training, he or she should be able to handle it for you.

And of course, this is a task that can be outsourced, should there simply not be adequate resources with your current accounts payable staff.

Regardless of the approach you choose, recognize the importance of the contact information and find a way to both collect and update it. As time goes on, it will become even more important in the accounts payable arena.

The Future of Vendor Portals

Vendor portals are all the rage now – at least in the press. When it comes to actual use in the corporate world, portals are not yet as popular. The first iteration of portals was a number of years ago. They were produced for the most part by very large companies for their own use. It is not surprising that more companies didn't follow suit as the cost for developing a portal is rumored to be in excess of a million US dollars. What's more, anytime there was an ERP upgrade, the programmers had to adjust the portal so it meshed with the newest features. But portals have come a long way since those expensive, albeit very useful, first introductions were unveiled.

Mixing Apples and Oranges

Talk to two different people, you'll get two different descriptions of what a vendor portal is and does. Make that ten people and you'll have ten distinct explanations. Part of the reason for this is that some folks use the term to describe an invoice automation vehicle, others use it to mean a master vendor file type function usually with a self-service feature and still others are talking about a place for vendors to check on their payment status.

So, when you hear the term vendor portal it is important to delve a little deeper to make sure you understand exactly what is being offered. Although those home-grown vehicles are still around, most frequently the portals today are developed by third parties and sold to numerous companies. This has dropped the price tremendously making them affordable to large numbers of big and mid-size companies and has mostly eliminated the ERP upgrade customization concern.

Customizable vs. Configurable

We say mostly because only a few companies choose to customize their installation. The service providers offering the portals have gotten savvy and most offer a configurable option so it is rarely necessary to customize, which drives the price up a good deal. If a company takes the configured approach, the service provider usually takes care of tweaking the portal when ERP upgrades are installed.

For this reason, companies are strongly advised against customizing an installation of a portal purchased from a third-party service provider. If you are considering having a portal purchased from a third-party service provider customized, think long and hard as to whether it is critical that you have that customization done. Is it really necessary for the running of an efficient operation or is it just something you'd like to have?

The cost factor is just one issue. If you choose to have the portal customized expect the installation time to increase significantly. While clearly no one knows the exact number of companies using portal technology, most experts estimate that somewhere between 70 and 90% of all companies are not using it. Thus, the market is wide open.

The Self-Service Feature

While most accounts payable departments are thrilled with the self-service feature inherent in many portals, the supplier community is less enthralled. Accounts payable departments like the self-service feature because it takes some of the work off their plates. Alas, it puts the responsibility for accurate information in the hands of the supplier.

As you might imagine, are not thrilled at the prospect of taking on the additional work. What's more most suppliers have thousands of customers so the prospect of having this additional work for most or all of their customers presents a daunting challenge.

So, there has been some pushback from the vendor community. What ultimately happens remains to be seen. But,

AP Now would not be surprised to see some changes being made to the self-service feature. While we expect a greater move to including the ability for vendors to check payment status online themselves, the same cannot be said for some of the other self-service implications, such as updating the master vendor file information.

The First Phase

Already there has been some changes in the vendor portal arena. We're seeing a consolidation of services. So, for example, some of the vendors who previously only offered an invoice automation feature are now scrambling to include the master vendor file feature and/or the self-service online payment status feature.

Those that are devoted to the master vendor file functionality do a lot more with it that is traditionally handled in master vendor file. Some track W-9s, some do TIN Matching, some do OFAC checking and some will periodically ping vendors to update their contact information. They are truly a master vendor file on steroids.

Some are doing this by merging with companies offering the feature they don't have and others are developing it themselves. Within the next few years, the portal that only offers one feature will be the oddity. It is expected that the survivors in this space will be those that find a way to include master vendor file functionality, invoice automation and the ability to check payment status online.

The Next Phase

At some point, and AP Now does not believe this will happen in the short term, vendor portals will be an integral part of any ERP system. They may start out as a bolt-on that end users will purchase separately, similar to the way they purchase some of the governance and risk functionality. However, we don't see this happening in the short term.

What's more, it is likely that when the big ERPs decide that portals compliment their existing business offerings, they will look to purchase one or more of the companies offering this technology rather than develop portals of their own.

Concluding Thoughts

So, thinking you'll wait for this eventuality is probably not a good interim strategy. Your organization will be left behind as others earn a competitive advantage by using an integrated portal functionality that integrates the three key elements of master vendor file, invoice automation and payment status. There are numerous service providers in this space all competing aggressively. It is important that when you decide to use this technology you evaluate your options carefully, for there is a lot of innovation going on in this space.

Chapter 8
Advances in Technologies Provide New Data Insights

Technology is making huge impacts on the way most people live their lives. It is having a similar impact on the business community and the accounts payable function is part of that upheaval. What's more with the plummeting of costs, it is now possible to analyze huge amounts of data without spending a small fortune. Tools are now available for mid-size companies and the average manager. In this chapter we examine:

- Affordable automation for the accounts payable function
- The use of scoreboards and dashboards to monitor accounts payable issues
- The explosion of Big Data into accounts payable and procure-to-pay
- The use of Data Analytics for payment, purchasing and other payables functions

Affordable Automation and Its Impact on AP

Once upon a time, automation in the business world was an expensive proposition. This was especially true for the accounts payable function, where projects often cost seven figures (or more) and took a long time to implement. All this has changed.

Current Environment

The cost of automation (like most technology) has plummeted bringing it within the reach of almost every organization. This is true over a wide variety of applications – including invoice processing. Complaints about expensive consultants needed to get a new application up and running are rarely heard.

Most of the applications available today for the accounts payable function do not require expensive outside consultants. In fact, they rarely involve more than a minimal participation from the organization's IT staff. Sometimes this can be as little as a few hours or days. Most of the work implementing the projects is being done by the vendor in concert with the accounts payable staff. The side benefit of this is that the people who will actually use the new system are the ones gaining the additional expertise during the implementation phase.

This translates into fewer consultants. In fact, most implementations do not rely on outside expertise, which of course, helps keep the cost down. If you are wondering how it is possible for the accounts payable staff to do the work that was done in the past by expensive outside consultants the answer is simple. Fewer organizations are choosing to customize the new applications. In the past this caused big problems anytime there was an upgrade in the ERP system.

Today over 90% of the organizations don't customize. Part of the reason they are able to do this is the applications offered generally include many configurable elements. Thus, the purchaser works within the framework of the new application without having to rely on expensive changes. This keeps the cost down as well as the implementation time.

Most of the new applications can be up and running in a matter of weeks, rather than months. It is not uncommon to hear of installations being completed in eight weeks (and occasionally shorter).

Cost

You may be thinking that all this is well and good but it is probably outside your budget. And, there's a good chance you'd be wrong. Here's why. Many of the applications today are offered on a service, or pay as you go basis. So, there is not a big up-front cost (that you didn't budget for) but rather a monthly or quarterly fee you pay as you use the application.

More than occasionally, you'll see a decrease in your outlay as the savings generated by the new process outpace the cost of using it. Of course, this depends on the application, your staffing requirements and a variety of other factors.

The chart below shows some of the automation applications currently available for accounts payable.

Some Automation Applications for AP

- e-invoicing
- Travel and Entertainment monitoring and processing
- Payment visibility (sometimes included in other products)
- Vendor portals
- Duplicate payment identification
- Electronic payments (through banks)
- e-mail (for sending and receiving pdfs of invoices)*
- IRS TIN Matching*

* Free

Blurring of Lines

The whole business world is evolving and the accounts payable function along with it. One of the trends that we've seen is the adoption by the bigger ERP systems of specialty applications. What starts as a specialty application is sometimes built into the main system in an upgrade or offered as an add-on function.

For example, many of the ERP systems now offer the ability to do some checking for duplicate payments before the payments are sent. There is also sophisticated software available to do this checking and of course, many companies have built their own routines using Excel and Access.

The salient point in this discussion is to investigate the complete functionality of your ERP system as it pertains to AP. You may have applications you don't know about. These are sometimes turned off during the initial instillation of the ERP and then never turned back on. Also, whenever there is an upgrade announced, check to see if there are some goodies in it to help with your accounts payable process.

The next place where we see a blurring of the lines involves personal devices. With the cost of new technology being more affordable than ever, a great number of business professionals have purchased their own smartphones and tablets. When they use them for work, the line between personal and professional becomes fuzzy.

This has spawned the BYOD (bring your own device) issue and is changing the way the corporate world views technology and security. What's more there are a whole slew of new issues that need to be addressed at the corporate level.

Implications for the AP Function

Clearly, automation has and will continue to make a big impact on the accounts payable function everywhere. This puts a new onus on professionals working in and managing the function to collect relevant information pertaining to the many automation options currently available. If you have the opportunity to go to a conference, take plenty of time to visit the vendor hall. Even if you don't go, look through the online listings to see who will be exhibiting and then check out their websites.

You can collect tons of information without ever leaving your office. Don't overlook the value of attending vendor webinars to learn what their products do. If you discover half way through that the product won't work for you, simple disconnect from the event.

The end result of the automation will mean the elimination of some transactional jobs. Of course, fewer jobs mean smaller departments, which can translate into some challenges when it comes to segregation of duties. However, it will also mean more time to spend on dispute resolution and other analytical tasks. Ultimately, it will mean a more efficient and effective accounts payable function.

There is last implication for the professionals who work in or manage the accounts payable function. The skillset needed to implement and continue to monitor for changing best practices, new frauds and increased regulatory requirements will be at a higher level thus raising the level and visibility of the entire accounts payable function.

Monitoring Progress in AP: Using Scorecards and Dashboards

A lot has been written in the last few years about analytics and Big Data in the accounts payable and procure-to-pay functions. Given the advances in technology and automation impacting most business functions, it's no surprise that there are now some nifty tools for monitoring performance and productivity. Let's take a look at the why, how and what of the measurement tools currently being used.

Why Should You Bother?

Peter Drucker has been quoted saying both "you can't manage what you can't measure" and "if you can't measure it, you can't improve it." Alas, he is correct, especially when it comes to accounts payable and procure-to-pay operations.

Not only is it important to measure your own productivity against the past, it is often insightful to measure it against others in the same industry or vertical. This is one way to determine whether your operations are truly as productive as they could be. Of course, the real trick is making sure that the benchmark you've decided to measure against is appropriate. It is not as easy as it might appear. But, that topic is for another time.

The Mechanics of Measurement

If you are lucky enough to be using an ERP system with a built in dashboard, take advantage of it. There's no reason to reinvent the wheel. Too often the dashboard functionality is either turned off or not fully utilized. If you have access to functionality like Oracle's WorkCenter, make sure you get everything you can out of it before developing your own separate dashboard or scorecard.

Dashboards and scorecards typically include both metrics and graphics and their goal is to give a snapshot picture of the operation. This enables management to track progress and productivity and identify potential problems before they develop into monumental headaches. These reports are also useful when it comes to tracking progress on new projects or initiatives.

Typically, they include key performance indicators (KPIs) which provide management insight into key ratios and other metrics they deem important. Sometimes, especially when there is a special project, a KPI will be included in the dashboard or on the scorecard for a period of time and then if there is no need to track that particular metric, it will be removed.

What Should You Measure

Typically, organizations will monitor both performance standards and metrics related to specific goals. The performance standards are used to measure how the staff is functioning. Some of the metrics might be related to individual processors while others relate to the performance of the group as a whole. Some sample performance metrics are shown in Table A below.

Table A. Sample Performance Metrics

- Number of invoices per processor
- Number of errors per processor
- Percentage of successful first time three-way matches
- Vendor payments with errors
- Number of duplicate payments
- Dollar amount of duplicate payments

- Number of early payment discounts lost
- Dollar amount of early payment discounts lost
- Number of invoices paid late
- Dollar amount of invoices paid late
- Number of inquiries into AP
- Number of Voided checks
- Number of vendors in master vendor file

Some organizations will share performance metrics with the staff as a way of motivating them. This can sometimes promote healthy competition among co-workers to see for example, who processed the most invoices in a given time period or better yet, who had the fewest errors. It is also useful to compare current metrics against past performance to see if the group is getting better or perhaps falling into some bad habits, which might, for example, cause the error rate to increase. An increase in the number of early payment discounts lost might signal a problem elsewhere that needs to be addressed.

In the current times, many accounts payable groups are taking on new projects. They may be trying to convert vendors to accept ACH payments or they may be trying to get vendors to submit invoices through a portal. Some of these goal related metrics are shown in Table B below. These projects can have their corresponding metrics included in the AP dashboard or scorecard.

Table B. Sample Goal Related Metrics

- Percent of vendors paid by ACH
- Percent of vendors paid by check
- Percent of vendors paid by p-card
- Percent of vendors paid by virtual card
- Percent of vendors sending email invoices
- Percent of vendors submitting invoices through a portal
- Number of Rush payments
- Percent of vendors with W-9s on file
- Percent W-9s successfully run through IRS TIN Matching

If the metrics aren't increasing the way they were projected to, there may be an issue that needs to be addressed. This is a simple way to monitor progress and where needed, have an executive get involved to rattle some chains. The data might give you the ammunition you need to get other departments and perhaps some vendors in line.

Don't be limited by the metrics shown here. If you have others that are relevant to your operations, by all means start tracking them.

Concluding Thoughts

So, whether you use a dashboard that is built into your ERP system, a scorecard that is automatically updated on a periodic but regular (daily, weekly, monthly etc.) basis, it is important that the intelligence be reviewed, shared and process changes made where needed as a result. For without such action, the dashboards and scoreboards will be of little value.

Use of Big Data in Accounts Payable and Procure-to-Pay (P2P)

Big data is all the rage now. Whether your organization is currently exploiting Big Data or not, it is critical that professionals working in accounts payable learn as much as possible about the ins and outs of Big Data. Here's why. It's not possible to pick up a publication targeting senior management without finding an article extoling the virtues of Big Data. These articles typically show impressive ROIs and huge bottom line improvements. The same goes for conferences focused on accountants, finance professionals and other senior level executives. It's not hard to understand why they come back from these events all fired up about Big Data.

What's more, many of the examples provided focus on topics like:

- Lost early payment discounts
- Duplicate payment identification
- Expense reimbursement
- Payment fraud

- Cleanup of the master vendor file
- Spend

The likelihood is high that when they turn their attention to Big Data, accounts payable will be in their crosshairs. When this happens, the savvy accounts payable professional is ready, armed with the latest information and a list of suggestions on how to make Big Data analytics work for their pet projects.

For once, you'll be able to make management happy by following their suggestions and achieve the goals that are high on your list of accomplishments. As a side benefit, if you are successful, you may get management to look at you and the accounts payable department in a new way. They may finally realize that there's some real talent in the department.

Big Data for All Companies

Big Data analytics gives us the facility to analyze extremely large and complex data sets that were previously beyond our competencies. It is believed that those companies that can take advantage of big data will have a competitive advantage. By being able to predict customer behavior, companies can change course and avoid being left with unwanted inventory. Recognizing the importance of big data, not only for inventory purposes but also in the accounts payable arena, leading edge companies are looking for ways to take advantage of this emerging technology. What follows is a three-part plan to help those hoping to benefit from big data analytics.

Step 1. Don't make the mistake of assuming the software needed costs a fortune putting it outside your reach. It doesn't have to. Look for SaaS (software as a service) options as well as those with low monthly flat fees.

Step 2. Once you've decided on your software, decide who will become your big data expert and train them. Some might argue that this step should be completed before a decision is made on software and we will not quibble with that approach. The important issue is to assign the responsibility to someone to be the point person to develop expertise in this area for your department.

Step 3 Decide on a strategy. What information are you looking for? What issues are you attempting to study? This may change over the course of time, especially as you see what is available and others learn of your expertise. But, having a good starting point is critical to making your big data project a success.

Getting Started with Big Data

As the cost of data storage plummets and we become more adept at collecting information about our vendors, our employees and our contract workers, the amount of information any accounts payable person can access is huge, if proper controls are not put in place. Not only do you have tax reporting information, but many accounts payable departments have their vendors' bank account information.

Clearly, we are not suggesting you don't collect this information; you need it to do a good job. But, we need to collect and monitor it intelligently. With regulatory compliance getting more complex it is inevitable that the issue of data and data protection will be one we all need to monitor. So, how can we intelligently set up a best practice approach to data collection and visibility?

- Step one: Don't forget about including appropriate segregation of duties into all your assignments.

- Step two: Make sure that you incorporate the appropriate privacy restrictions around data. Most of us collect tax reporting information, some of it personal data. We need to set up our processes so only those who need this data can see it. It should be masked to anyone else. With the concerns about identity theft we owe this to our vendors, employees and contractors.

- Step three: Ensure that there is an audit trail so should there be a problem at some point, you can see who accessed the information and when.

- Step four: Make sure employees understand they should limit their queries to those related to their position and not go on an exploration to see what's in the files of others.

The Big Data Skillset Issue

Here's the situation. Computing capabilities have been doubling every two years since the mid-sixties. This phenomenon was first observed and documented by Gordon Moore, co-founder of Intel. Of course in his case he was talking about transistors on integrated circuits. Most experts have expanded his theory, referred to as Moore's Law, to processing speed and memory capacity. Remarkably, his prediction has stood the test of time.

What this means in today's accounts payable function is that today we've got a tremendous amount of data as well as the computing power to analyze it. And best of all, the price for this amazing capability has plummeted as well. The oft-quoted statistic from a McKinsey report that "it costs less than $600 to buy a disk drive with the capacity to store all of the world's music" demonstrates just how low the prices have fallen. It also proves that computing capacity of this magnitude is within the reach of virtually every organization.

Alas, while computing power has been exploding along with the data generated by our systems there is one factor that has not kept up with this explosion. And that is our ability to analyze what is commonly referred to as Big Data. There is a definite shortfall is this area.

Professionals with the ability to effectively analyze big data will be in big demand in the coming years.

Spend Analytics and How AP Fits In

When it comes to data, accounts payable has more than most

people realize. Unfortunately, it often does nothing with that information except when it can help the accounts payable process directly. It is fine to use the data to improve accounts payable and you should. But, if that is the extent the data is used, you're only getting a small piece of the benefits that could be gotten from the data. It's like buying a television set and then only watching the shows on one channel.

Visibility into Spend

The purchasing department could benefit significantly by mining the data accounts payable has in its system. By working with purchasing to extract the data, accounts payable might also improve its relationship with that department. Let's take a look at some of the data that purchasing might be able to use.

1. A comparison of purchases from the same vendor, of the same item, by different locations at different prices. If purchasing had all this information, it would be able to negotiate the best price for all locations. What's more, by combining the information into one contract, additional quantity discounts might be arranged.

2. A comparison of purchases from the different vendors, of the same item, by different locations at different prices. If purchasing had this important pricing information, it might be able to direct all purchases to the vendor offering the lowest price. And as above, by combining the information into one contract, additional quantity discounts might be arranged.

3. A comparison of purchases from the same or different vendors, of the same item, by different locations at the same price but with different terms. If purchasing had this important information about different terms, it might be able to direct all purchases to the vendor offering the best terms. And as above, by combining the information into one contract, additional quantity discounts might be arranged.

These are just a few examples. A conversation with purchasing about the data available might result in additional scenarios put forth by the purchasing department. This is a win-win for everyone. For, if purchasing is able to negotiate better contracts, the savings goes straight to the bottom line resulting in a more profitable organization. And, that can't hurt at raise time.

Controlling Maverick Spend: How Analytics Can Help

Just about every company has them. They are the folks who sometimes intentionally and sometimes not, throw a monkey wrench into the corporate spend policy by not following the guidelines. Occasionally, there is fraud involved but more often than not, that is not the case. Many refer to this spend as maverick spend and the folks who create these problems (at least in the United States) as cowboys. Maverick spend typically results from one of the following three:

1. Purchases made from a supplier other than a preferred supplier, even if at a lower cost.
2. Purchases made without going through procurement, even though they should have.
3. Purchases made under questionable circumstances, either from a related source or at a higher price. It is this last category that is most likely to involve a fraudulent transaction.

Occasionally, folks from the first category who have made purchases at a lower cost are left scratching their heads wondering what they did wrong. What they fail to realize is that while the individual purchase may have been at an attractive price, it could result in a higher price for other purchases made under the preferred contract, if promised levels are not made.

So, what can you do to control this behavior?

- **Step1**. Set up clear policies defining procurement practices.

- **Step2**. Identify your maverick spend. This is where your data analytics will come in handy.
- **Step3**. Immediately, notify the appropriate managers so that the maverick behavior can be stopped.

Stopping maverick spend as soon as the cycle starts is critical. In its Report to the Nations, The Association of Certified Fraud Examiners reports that on average, occupational (employee) corruption schemes run for an average of 18 months. The economic damage that can be done in that timeframe can be severe and the money rarely recovered.

Therefore it is important that the data analytics be run on a very regular basis, either weekly or monthly. If you only look at your data annually, say at budget time, maverick behavior may go on for a long time doing real damage to your preferred contracts or worse. Weekly or monthly is better.

Other Data Analytics Project Any AP Department Can and Should Do

While most everyone likes to get money back, it can sometimes be a sign that all is not right in your operation. We're talking about vendor credits and while a few are to be expected, a higher number of them could signal a problem. Your first step in figuring out if you have a problem is to identify vendors with a high number of vendor credits. Periodically run take a look at outstanding vendor credits. You can do this by running analytics but you also should be getting statements from vendors on a regular basis and checking for open credits you don't have on your books.

Once you've got your data, make a list of the vendors with the most credits. You can start with your top ten or twenty five depending on the nature of your operations. Then analyze to see if one of the following conditions exists.

1. Is the processor associated with this account making too many errors?

2. Is the supplier in question sending poor quality product?

3. Is the vendor making too many mistakes on invoices?

4. Are your purchase orders accurate?

5. Are you taking vendor credits in a timely manner or letting them languish?

6. Do you have an unethical employee?

7. Do you have another problem?

People sometimes wonder how vendor credits can signal an unethical employee. If one of your workers colludes with an employee at your supplier, they can mistakenly make an overpayment and then request the credit be paid back with a check. By intercepting the check, cashing it and then splitting the money, neither of the companies would be the wiser. This is just one more reason why every company should make as many payments electronically as possible. While this is less of a problem for most Europeans, Americans have a lot of catching up to do in this regard.

Chapter 9:

Unexpected Challenges Created by Personal Devices

(Smartphone, Tablets and Who Knows What Else)

An ever-growing number of professionals are stepping up their personal technology game through the use of smartphones and tablets. They are purchasing these devices with their own funds. In addition to using them for personal matters, some dedicated employees are bringing them to work to improve their workplace efficiency. And, that is where one of the newest issues facing accounts payable lies. Unless this matter is addressed adequately, these employees are unintentionally introducing additional risk into the payment and data stream of the organization. In this piece we take a look at what that risk is and how every organization can deal with it.

The Issue

The Bring Your Own Device (BYOD) issue raises concern because most individuals do not have the same level of security on these devices as their employers put on the computers used by employees for their day-to-day tasks. Even if the virus protections are strong when the devise is new, few regularly update them.

These devices are being used by some employees to access and respond to e-mail, access the ERP system to update company financial and accounting records and access bank balance reporting and payment systems. It's not only the organization's data that is at risk, it's also their bank accounts.

The Decision

Many organizations have yet to address this issue. That is a huge mistake. Every organization needs to examine the issue and decide how to handle this issue. Those who have addressed it typically decide on one of the following strategies:

- They forbid employees from using personal devices for any work associated with the organization;
- They allow employees to use personal devices for work associated with the organization, only after the employee has brought the devise to IT so the appropriate security software can be loaded onto it;
- They give employees the choice of an allowance towards the purchase of a personal device or using one provided by the organization.

Those that choose the last strategy also make it clear to employees that if they take the allowance, the IT staff will not help them with any technical issues they might have. They are on their own with that. Clearly, the organizations that take this approach would prefer that employees took the devise they were offering. However, many employees complain about having to carry around two phones, a laptop and perhaps a tablet as well. So, the allowance approach is a compromise on that front.

Whatever the path an organization chooses, it needs to have a formal policy in place for all its employees.

The Policy

Before deciding on a corporate wide policy, all affected parties should be consulted. This may seem obvious, but more often than not, policies are set by top management and/or HR. In this case, it is critical that IT be included in the discussion. It also might not be a bad idea to include someone who fully understands how electronic payment fraud is committed and what needs to be done to stop it.

Once the decision has been made as to which path the organization intends to take, the policy should be communicated to all employees. Don't overlook the importance of sharing the decision that employees should NOT use personal devices for company business. If this is the path your organization chooses, it needs to be clearly communicated.

Issues to be Covered

At a minimum, the policy should address the following:

- Whether personal devices can be used;
- If personal devices are allowed, what steps the employee must take before using the devise for company activities;
- How much, if anything, the company is willing to pay towards the purchase of the device;
- How much, if anything, the company is willing to pay towards monthly charges;
- Instructions on whether the device can be used for company business utilizing public open access internet connectivity (say in airports or local coffee shops);
- How frequently virus protection software should be updated;
- What to do if the device is lost or stolen;
- If the company paid for all or part of the device, what happens to it when the employee leaves the company;
- What happens to data that might be on the device when the employee leaves the company (including company e-mail mailboxes);
- Any limitations as to which devices can be used to access which resources (for example, maybe the organization would prefer company bank accounts not be accessed with smartphones);
- Guidelines as to what an employee should do if he or she thinks their device has been compromised.

Other Considerations

In addition to policies for employees, every organization

allowing the use of personal devices needs to put in place procedures to ensure the program runs smoothly. It will need to decide the following:

- Whether use of personal devices is monitored at the corporate level, the departmental level or both;
- Who will track that all devices are regularly updated with the latest security protocols;
- Who is responsible for updating policies and procedures for employees;
- Practices to ensure devices are retrieved (if that is the policy) when an employee leaves the company;
- Protocols for removing company data from devices owned by employees who leave the company;
- What, if any, periodic reporting should be done regarding number of devices, level of use etc.;
- Who will be responsible for reviewing departmental policies regarding use of personal devices to ensure that at a minimum they meet corporate guidelines.

This is a new and evolving area. The issues related to it are just starting to emerge. We fully expect this topic to not only develop more nuances but become one of those standard issues every organization addresses. However, we are probably a few years away from that.

How Smartphones and Tablets Are Impacting AP

AP Now recently conducted a survey to determine how personal devices were impacting the functionality of the accounts payable process. This is important not only as it pertains to understanding how the function operates now and in the future but also the impact on internal controls and fraud. Today, virtually every professional has a smartphone. These can be iphones, Blackberries or one of the many adroids on the market. Ownership of tablets, while high, is not quite as high. Possession of a smartphone or tablet does not mean that it is being used professionally, which is where the control and fraud concerns arise. Let's take a look at how these devices are being used.

Who Paid for the Phone

After ascertaining that smartphones are a common commodity among the folks working in and managing accounts payable, we then set out to determine whether these were intended to be used personally or professionally or both. Just over 24% of the phones were paid for by the employers of the folks who operated them. This figure is up considerably over the last time AP Now asked this question.

Two-thirds of those using employer-paid for smartphones can check personal e-mail on those devices, although only 35% actually do check personal e-mail on them.

Of those who paid for the cell phones themselves, just over 72% have the ability to check work e-mail on them, with slightly over half (56%) actually checking work e-mail on their personal cell phone.

Who Paid for the Tablets

While tablets are not as common as smartphones, close to 80% of the professionals working in and managing accounts payable have one. Just over 20% of the tablets were paid for by the employers of the folks who operated them.

Less than 15% of those using employer-paid tablets check personal e-mail on those devices. However, of those who paid for the tablets themselves, about 60% check work e-mail on their personal tablets.

Online Banking

Probably one of the biggest concerns regarding the use of personal devices for business functions revolves around the use of these devices for online banking activities. For without the same high level fraud prevention protocols that are used on desktop computers, use of a personal device could open the company to a risk it never intended to assume.

Just under 4% of the survey respondents who purchased

tablets themselves use them regularly for online banking activities. Almost 8% do so on an occasional basis. If the proper protections have been put in place on these tablets, this is fine. If not, the potential for problems exists.

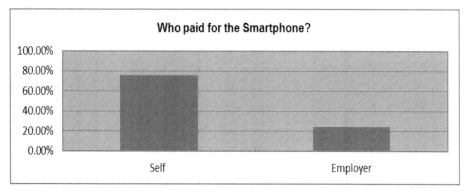

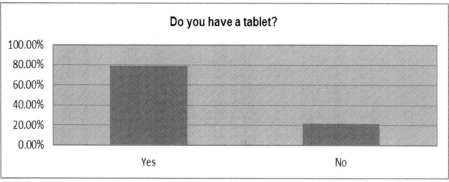

Implications for Accounts Payable

Smartphones and tablets are no longer novelty gadgets used by a few techy professionals. Not only do we see them on TV shows, they can now be found in many leading-edge accounts payable departments. Our goal is to find ways to take advantage of this technology in ways that will make the function more efficient without weakening the needed controls around the function.

Believe it or not, the first step is to determine exactly how many of your employees are using these devices for company work. The number may be higher than you suspect. One organization was dumbfounded to find that it had twice the number of devices connected to its systems as it had registered.

This means that even at those organizations with good policies regarding personal devices, a large number of rogue employees could be using their devices without the necessary fraud and anti-virus protocols. Typically this happens because the employees don't realize they were supposed to get permission to use their devices, have their anti-virus protections regularly updated and don't understand the risks involved.

Concluding Thoughts

Personal devices will continue to play a role in the way the accounts payable department functions. It is critical that we find the best ways to use these devices without weakening controls and increasing risk.

How Some Companies Are Implementing BYOD Policies

With the use of personal devices in business exploding, organizations everywhere are starting to develop policies regarding their use for company business. As part of a recent survey, AP Now asked its readers about their company policies regarding use of the device, who pays for the device, security on the device and a few other issues. While some limit the definition of device in this context to cell phones and tablets, others include laptops. What we found was there is no one approach or policy that is being used across the board. What follows is a look at some of the aspects of BYOD (bring your own device) policies currently being used at the organizations that employ the survey respondents.

Use of a Device

The first issue to be considered is whether use of a personal device for company business is even permitted. Some who allow limited use will limit that to e-mail. Here's what readers told us about use of a device at their organizations:

- Remote devices are not encouraged but permitted.
- A maximum of two devices per user can be configured

- Remote access on an unapproved device is only support through a remote portal
- Case managers and employees working with clients are required to use employer device to comply with HIPAA regulations.

Who Gets A Device

Although it would seem that personal devices are just that; personal, some companies do pay for their employees' devices. There is wide divergence on this issue. Here's how one company addresses the who-gets-a-company-paid-for-device-and-who-doesn't issue.

- Only traveling employees are required to use their personal phones for company work and they receive a monthly phone stipend to cover those costs. Employees who occasionally travel can only submit for reimbursement roaming charges incurred during business travel.

Who Pays the Monthly Fees

Regardless of who paid for the device, if it is used more than occasionally for company business, there is the question of the monthly usage fees. Again, there is no consistency in what's happening in the marketplace. Here are the policies in use by a few of the survey respondents' organizations:

- We reimburse at a flat rate for BYOD for individuals with a verified business requirement for occasional remote access to email. The employee is responsible for responsible for monitoring the data usage and ensuring they have selected an appropriate data plan. Employees are required to advise the company if they are able to obtain a plan for less than the corporate rate.

- Employee will not be reimbursed for devices they own personally.

- The employer pays monthly allowance for exempt employees to use personal device for work.

Security Policies

This is one area where some consistency is emerging, although to be clear, this is only emerging at companies where there is a policy. The recognition that these devices need to be secured is fast becoming commonplace. How that is done varies widely as you can see from the policies shown below.

- We have to load software and password protection to our device.
- Device must support remote wipe capabilities
- Device must natively support encryption.
- Device must have a strong password.
- Password must be changed every 90 days.
- Regardless if the device is owned by the company or the employee, it is required to have the password unlock feature to gain access to the device. It must also comply with company standards.
- The company will set up all personal devices to access work email if the employee so wishes.

Other Restrictions

Because this is an evolving issue, there are many facets to it. What's more what one company sees as an issue is of no concern to the next. What follows are some of the additional policies related to personal devices as reported by the survey respondents.

- Use of personal devices is limited to email and instant messaging. Strong policy against transfer/storage of company data in personal devices. Company has provided tablets to some senior executives and field workers, not to most office staff.
- If the company has issued a device, the employee is allowed occasional use only and that use must not require large bandwidth. If the employee uses a

personally-owned device, the employer is allowed to remotely wipe device if a problem occurs.
- Company data cannot be downloaded on personal devices. Also on company owned devices any software installed must be run through the IT department or be approved by IT before it is loaded onto the device. Applications such as Log Me In are not allowed.
- Company work can only be performed on company owned equipment.
- Devices provided to employees only, not independent contractors or others doing work on behalf of the company.
- Only allowed through company approved apps

Concerns Some Firms Have about the Exploding Use of BYODs by Their Employees

Given the hybrid nature of personal devices used for business purposes, it's not surprising that many companies approach the BYOD (bring your own device) issue with some trepidation. The successful ones don't stick their heads in the sand, but rather identify their concerns and then develop processes to control the risks surrounding those matters. It's similar to driving your car to the mall. You stay home because you're afraid someone will steal the car while you're shopping. Instead, you lock it up when you get there.

What follows is a look at the major concerns our readers have expressed in relation to the BYOD issue along with suggested approaches for dealing with the matter.

Concerns

Whether company data is obtained by hackers who exploit security weaknesses in a personal device or a device containing proprietary company information is lost or stolen, the potential damage is the same. You can guard against hackers by insisting all personal devices have strong anti-virus software installed and regularly updated. Whatever protocols are used on employees' desktop computers should be used on personal devices. Security should be just as tight.

As for lost or stolen devices, if the company is using a mobile device management solution then it's possible to remotely wipe a device. This is the best response to this threat. Of course, it only works if the employee is aware the device is missing and notifies the company promptly.

• **Fraud risks**. Loss of data, while important, isn't the only risk associated with use of personal devices for company business. When devices are used to access banking information online, there are potentially additional complications. The same is true if the device is used to initiate or approve or release payments. These include wired transfers and electronic payments.

There are two ways to address the financial risk associated with personal devices. The first is to put restrictions in your policy prohibiting employees from using personal devices for company banking activities. Enforcing such a policy is difficult and not without its challenges, so clearly not a 100% solution.

The second is to ensure the devices have the most-current anti-virus protection software on them. This will make it as difficult to penetrate the personal device as it is to infiltrate a desktop computer. Of course, the devices also need to be password protected to help in case of theft and mobile device management solutions will also add a layer of protection.

• **Ownership of devices**. When employees pay for the devices completely, the ownership issue is quite clear. But many organizations are now giving an allowance toward the purchase of the device. Then the matter gets a little sticky. For starters, who owns the phone number and who is responsible if or when the device is lost or stolen.

Lost or stolen devices can lead to requests for reimbursement and then the issue is how much is the organization liable for. By clearly addressing this issue up-front and spelling it out in writing for employees there should be little conflict. A clearly defined policy should minimize this type of problem for most organizations. Of course, this will only work if the policy is shared with all employees. Also, it has to be enforced across the board. If you make an exception for one employee, others will find out and expect similar treatment.

• **How devices are used**. Part of the reason so many employees use their personal devices for business purposes is the desire to carry only one device. Yet the use of the same device for both personal and company business can cause a conflict between how the employee intends to use the device and what the company wishes to allow to be done with it.

The first "debate" often centers around texting. This will be especially true if you have many younger employees using devices for company business. For them, texting is a way of life. Many companies have strict no (or very limited) text messaging policies. Clearly, if the employee texts frequently restrictions on this feature will become an issue.

Some organizations restrict usage of these devices to approving invoices or expense reports but are not for processing company payments online. This includes approving or releasing the payments at the bank.

Note: Some companies allow employee to add the app 'Good' to their personal devices so they can view company e-mails etc. and can carry only one device. There have been complaints about this app but upon investigation it appears that the complaints should really be focused on the limitations the company in question has put on the app and not the app itself.

• **Unauthorized access.** In most instances, when an employee uses a personal device to access either company e-mail, the organization's online banking facilities or its ERP system, it should be done with approval. And the approval should be spoken or written and not implied.

Unfortunately, even companies with strong policies in place find that they have more use of personal devices than they are aware of. More often than not, there is no malice involved just employees finding ways to be more efficient, without realizing they are weakening the controls around the process. Good communication with employees should make a dent in this problem, although I suspect it is one that will be with us for a long time.

• **Access limitations.** What type of corporate data can be accessed from a personal device will vary from employee to employee depending on the nature of their job. For example maybe you are willing to allow employees to access their e-mail but not your ERP system or data that has HIPAA restrictions.

Similar restrictions should surround banking information. Privacy is a huge issue when it comes to data. The restrictions on access that are in place for your main operations should follow to the personal devices.

• **Data ownership.** While the ownership issue might be quite clear in some cases, it can get a bit tricky in others. This matter needs to be thought through thoroughly. Some organizations automatically wipe the company e-mail accounts and phone directories from employees' devices when the employee separates from the company.

But what about personal phone numbers stored on the device? Do they get wiped in the process? The same can be said for Word or Excel files. If the employee paid for the device completely, does the company have the legal right to wipe data from it? These are all issues that need to be reviewed and incorporated into a corporate policy.

This issue is a relatively new one and as such it is very likely more factors will emerge as time goes on. There is no right or wrong policy on many of these concerns. How each is handled will be part of the larger corporate policy.

Every organization will need to decide how they'd like to move forward. With all the new technology coming out and the way the accounts payable function is increasingly becoming more automated, effective BYOD policies are critical. What's more, like everything else, the policy will need to be revisited frequently to ensure it meets all the organization's needs. New unforeseen problems will crop up from time to time and they will have to be addressed and incorporated into the policy.

Concluding Thoughts

Smartphones, laptops and tablets are clearly here to stay. It is critical for every organization to establish a policy limiting and guiding their use for company business. As part of that policy the employee should be informed what, if anything, will happen should the employee and the organization part ways. But don't rest once you've established a policy for the devices discussed. Advances in technology almost guarantee that before long there will be some new device that must be integrated into the policy. Have you thought about how your policy will need to be adjusted to accommodate employee purchases of Apple watches or Google glasses?

Chapter 10

Often-Overlooked
Internal Control Breakdowns

We're not saying that internal control breakdowns are new; heavens knows, they've been with accounts payable since the day after the first accounts payable function was set up. What is new is the different places internal control breakdowns are being discovered. While we are fairly certain the breakdowns are for the most part, not new, we do believe that in many of the cases discussed, they have gone undetected for years.

Most accounts payable, procure-to-pay, accounting, finance, auditing and treasury professionals are well aware that strong internal controls are the first step towards safeguarding the organization's assets. When it comes to accounts payable, these controls guard against duplicate payments, erroneous payments and fraudulent payments.

In this section we start by looking at why controls sometimes fail before moving onto the segregation of duties issue. This is a growing concern as accounts payable departments become smaller thanks to advances in technology. While it's great that the technology and automation reduce costs, the fallout from that issue is that sometimes departments become so small, they no longer can incorporate appropriate segregation of duties. What was once a small company issue has become a concern for a growing number of organizations.

Then we drill down into the nitty-gritty of the function and identify internal control breakdowns related to:

- The Payment Process
- The People
- The Process

Why Internal Controls Sometimes Fail

More than occasionally controls fail, not because someone is deceitful but rather due to a lack of understanding of the principles or how they should be implemented. Let's take a look at five common reasons internal controls fail.

Reason #1: Lack of appropriate review. This happens frequently with approvers signing expense reimbursement reports. Unfortunately, it also sometimes happens with purchasers approving invoices for payment.

Solution: Make managers responsible for what they approve - really. A few organizations have gone so far as to make it a firing offense if a manager approves an obviously fraudulent expense reimbursement. Most are not willing to go that far. Some are making it a matter for consideration when calculating the annual salary increase.

Reason #2: Incomplete segregation of duties. When it comes to processing invoices for payment, it is critical that no one person can perform more than one leg of the operation. For example, someone shouldn't have the ability to enter invoices and sign checks. Too often we see companies set up the segregation of duties correctly and then make one or two "exceptions," usually for a trusted employee such as the controller or accounts payable manager. Smaller accounts payable departments are sometimes challenged when it comes to setting up processes so duties are appropriately segregated.

Solution: The first step is to realize that there can be no exceptions when it comes to separating duties. Remember internal fraud is most likely to be committed by a long term trusted employee. Regardless of the operational efficiencies that can be achieved by allowing these exceptions, the more important issue of fraud protection should override. So, allow no exceptions. Smaller organizations sometimes have to look outside accounts payable to help. Some common examples of segregating duties by taking advantage of help from other departments include putting the master vendor file elsewhere in accounting and having Treasury responsible for getting signatures put on checks (if they are not signed as part of the check printing cycle).

Reason #3: Incomplete knowledge regarding policies and procedures. Too often we don't realize that the knowledge we have regarding how the accounts payable department operates has been accumulated over a long period of time. When newcomers are hired, they are typically given a day or two of training before being hurled into the mix to sink or swim. Most do a fairly good job but occasionally do miss a fine point or a procedure that only comes up once in a blue moon.

Solution: Probably the best approach any organization can take when it comes to ensuring complete knowledge about policies and procedures is to have a detailed, up-to-date policy and procedures manual. Give this to every processor as a reference guide and they can check it when those odd transactions show up. Encourage even your seasoned staff to refer to the guide when they are not 100% certain how something should be handled. Refresher training is another step you can also take to ensure you don't run into this problem.

Reason #4: Sharing passwords. It is quite tempting when an employee is heading out for vacation to ask that employee to share his/her password with another employee who will take over the vacationing employee's responsibility. Resist the temptation. This is a slippery slope and whether sharing a password for a vacation or on a regular basis, it is a bad idea. It completely obliterates the audit trail making it impossible to tell who did what.

Solution: The answer is obvious. When someone needs to take over the responsibilities of another employee, set them up with their own password. When the vacation is over and if you don't need/want that employee to have access, cancel the access. This may be an extra step but it protects your internal controls.

Reason #5: Overrides. Management overrides of transactions are an easy way to fix mistake. Unfortunately, they are also an easy way for an unscrupulous employee to adjust the records to cover up a fraud.

Solution: If at all possible, do not use management overrides to fix a problem. Go through the more laborious route of doing the correct accounting to take care of the issue, even if it means owning up to some really stupid mistakes. If your organization does not want to go that route and insists on allowing overrides, then at a minimum have a form explaining the reason for the override and have it signed by at least one executive other than the person putting through the override.

Internal controls are an important component of any organization's fraud prevention program. They also go a long way to helping ensure accurate records and financial statements. Don't let the senseless issues discussed above get in the way of your controls. Implement the solutions suggested to strengthen your controls rather than weaken them.

Problems Created by Inappropriate Segregation of Duties

One of the principles related to strong internal controls is the appropriate segregation or separation of duties. When it comes to the procure-to-pay cycle, this means that no one person should have the ability to perform more than one piece of the transaction. By restricting this access it becomes more difficult for an employee to defraud the organization. Typically, collusion makes a fraud easier to commit. With the same person handling two or more legs of a transaction, the collusion is a done deal. What follows is a look at the different pieces of the procure-to-pay function. This is followed by identifying ten situations ripe with conflict of interest and weakened internal controls.

Dissecting the Procure-to-Pay Process

Typically there are three distinct departments involved in the procure-to-pay operation of any company. They are the purchasing department, the receiving department and the accounts payable department. Rarely do the responsibilities handled in one department overlap into a second. However, organizations with smaller accounts payable or purchasing functions may sometimes find themselves stretched to assign tasks in such a way that there are no segregation of duties issues.

Before we look at some of the potential problems that might arise if duties aren't separated appropriately, let's take a look at the different steps along the procure-to-pay trail. Most companies have different parties handling each of the following:

1. Ordering goods

2. Approving purchases

3. Receiving ordered materials

4. Approving invoices for payment

5. Processing invoices

6. Handling preprinted check stock

7. Signing checks/releasing ACH payments

8. Setting up vendors/change vendor information in the Master Vendor File

9. Handling Unclaimed Property reporting

10. Reviewing and reconciling financial records including bank recs

Where Controls Break Down

When two or more legs of the transaction are handled by the same person, there can be a problem. Now, for example, if an organization had one individual ordering goods and doing the unclaimed property reporting, there wouldn't be much of an issue. The problem is the skillset needed to do those two tasks are so disparate that no organization would have the same person performing them. The problem occurs with tasks that are in the same chain. Let's take a look at what can go wrong when certain responsibilities are handled by the same individual.

Potential Conflict #1: If the same person orders goods and then approves the purchases, there is no control and no checks and balances. Of course, the person who ordered the goods might have to review the purchase to ensure that what is on the invoice is what was ordered and not something entirely different.

Potential Conflict #2: If the same individual orders and receives purchases, there is no control over whether the goods were actually ordered in the first place. All an employee who wanted to defraud the company would have to do would be to send an invoice and claim it had been received. Alternatively, low-quality goods could be ordered while the invoice might reflect the price of much higher priced materials.

Potential Conflict #3: If the same person received goods and approved invoices for payment there would be no controls over the pricing or quality.

Potential Conflict #4: If the same individual approved purchases and set up vendors in master vendor file, it would be very easy to set up a phony vendor and submit a fraudulent invoice for goods that do not go through the companies receiving channel.

Potential conflict: #5: If the same individual could approve invoices and process invoices, there would be no controls in place to ensure the invoice was legitimate to start with. The crook would submit and approve a phony invoice and then the processor would run it through allegedly verifying it.

Potential conflict #6: By allowing the same person to process invoices and set up vendors in the master vendor file you open the door to someone setting up a phony vendor in the master vendor file and then processing an invoice against it as though it had been approved by a purchaser.

Potential conflict #7: Permitting one person to both process invoices and sign checks or release ACH payments, you are removing the checks and balances put in place to prevent an employee from processing a phony invoice or sending it to the wrong address.

Potential conflict #8: If one individual can approve invoices and set up vendors in the master vendor file, they can set up a phony vendor, submit a phony invoice and then approve it for payment. When the approved invoice shows up in accounts payable, the processor won't really know if they are handling a fraudulent invoice and it will fly through your process – especially if it is for a non-PO item.

Potential conflict #9: if the same person handles preprinted check stock and signs checks, they are effectively set up with a blank company check.

Potential conflict #10: If the same person reconciles the bank account statements and handle unclaimed property reporting, they will know which checks haven't cleared. This will enable them to easily adjust the records so when the unclaimed property is turned over to the state, it is reported in their name instead of the rightful owner's name. The company's records will balance and unless the rightful owner comes forward (unlikely) the employee will claim the money that did not belong to them and no one will be the wiser.

Concluding Thoughts

Inappropriate segregation of duties is one sign of weak internal controls. We've uncovered ten of them above but you can probably come up with a lot more. Now, some organizations just don't have enough people working in accounts payable and purchasing to implement all the separations discussed above. They have two options.

1) Enlist employees in other departments to handle some of the responsibilities discussed. It is not uncommon to find master vendor file, bank reconciliations and/or unclaimed property handled in another department so the appropriate segregation of duties is maintained.

2) If help is not available from other departments, it is sometimes necessary to add additional steps in the process to make up for the weakened controls. This might be the president or CFO reviewing all checks before they are released in a smaller company.

The important issue is that an organization recognizes where there potential weaknesses are and create additional reviews around them.

Internal Controls Breakdown: The Payment Process

Strong internal controls are the underpinning of a payment process that doesn't leak profits and runs as efficiently as possible. They are a big component in any fraud prevention program and as an added bonus, go a long way in preventing duplicate payments. But occasionally, controls break down. This most typically happens when the process in question is something outside the norm. A company may have great controls for the bulk of its transactions but those one-offs and infrequent transactions can cause control problems if thought is not given to incorporating good processes for those rare occasions. When it comes to payments this can happen in three arenas; wire transfers, payments made outside accounts payable and with recurring payments. Let's take a look at each.

Wire Transfers

Traditionally, wire transfers were made when the payment

amount was large and/or the payment was going across borders from one country to another. With the growing use of ACH some of the wire activity has migrated away to the ACH arena. Wire transfers are relatively expensive and usually result in same day availability of funds, if the transaction is domestic. They are made just as often outside of accounts payable as they are by individuals working in accounts payable.

The issue is complicated by the fact that often wire payments are made for not-purchase order items. So, instructing organizations to use the proverbial three-way match and make sure POs and receivers are extinguished (one of the best ways to prevent duplicate payments of PO related invoices) is worthless. Since these payments are often for large dollar amounts, a duplicate payment is this arena can be costly indeed.

Very occasionally, a wire transfer will be made to cover a rush payment for an invoice that was not paid on time. When this is done, it is critical that the three-way match be completed and the purchase order and receiving document extinguished.

Here are a few controls you can add to your process to ensure wire transfers are paid only once:

1) Make sure there is adequate backup for each wire transfer, even though no three-way match is being completed. This way should someone suspect a duplicate there will be sufficient information to make that determination.

2) If possible, limit the payment type for particular vendors to one type (wire, ACH, check or p-card). If attempts are made to use another payment type, have the system alert the processor.

3) Periodically review the accounts of vendors typically paid by wire. This might include loan payments, interest payments, and leases.

4) Alert processors to vendors who are usually paid by wire so they can thoroughly research any invoice that comes in for

payment using another payment vehicle.

5) Periodically run your list of wires against lists of other payments made looking for duplicates. Research any potential duplicates.

You should note that many payment auditors will automatically perform the last step as part of their recovery efforts.

Payments Made outside Accounts Payable

While wires in many companies have always been made outside accounts payable, traditionally they were the only payments not made by the accounts payable staff. Since the items covered by wires were usually pretty easy to identify, the chances of a duplicate payment slipping through were not high, assuming the organization took a few basic steps to protect itself.

The advent of ACH is changing that situation. They are cheaper than both wire transfers and paper checks and appear to be the wave of the future for corporations making payments. Approximately, 20% of all organizations have ACH payments initiated outside of accounts payable. Since the items being paid by ACH are the same as the items being paid by the accounts payable staff, problems can arise under a few circumstances. If the outside staff does not use the same strong rigid controls used by accounts payable, duplicate payments will arise. Specifically this means the staff outside accounts payable must:

1) use the same rigid coding standards used in AP;

2) perform the three-way match; and

3) extinguish purchase orders and receivers once the payment has been made.

If they do not follow the same standards, and an invoice appears in accounts payable, it will be paid, for the staff will have no way of knowing it had already been addressed. Thus it is imperative that those organizations making payments outside accounts payable sufficiently train the staff making those payments so duplicates don't slip through.

Recurring and Repetitive Payments

There are a whole variety of items that require the same payment to be made every month. This might include things like rent, equipment leases, loan payments etc. Depending on your industry, there might be other items as well. Rather than create a new voucher each month for the same exact payment, some organizations set these items up to be automatically paid on a recurring basis.

If care is not taken and an end date included in the arrangement, the organization could find itself paying for something it no longer was obliged to pay for. Hence it is critical that when recurring payments are set up, an end date be included rather than have them go on without a light at the end of the tunnel.

The second problem that can occur is when the item is paid off early. In the case of a loan this might be an early payment or a renegotiation to get a lower rate. In the case of a lease, occasionally the lessor will entice the lessee into a new lease for better/newer equipment or whatever. Both of these situations are fine as long as the initial payment is stopped when the new payment stream begins. More than occasionally this does not happen and the original payment continues as well as the new payment.

You can run into the same problem with repetitive payments for services, phones etc. If someone does stay on top of these accounts the organization can find itself paying for services never used. For example, if the phone company isn't notified when a phone line is no longer needed, it will continue to bill for it. For most organizations this isn't a problem as it uses all its phone lines. But those who have a significant downsizing initiative may find themselves paying for services not being used. The same can be said for subscriptions, online services, and specialized database access for employees who have left (voluntarily or not).

Strong internal controls protect any organization. It is important to make sure yours cover not only the functions used on a regular basis but also those only used occasionally.

The Internal Controls Breakdown: The Overlooked People Issues

Some of our internal controls breakdowns occur in often-overlooked people issues. They are either tasks we forget to do or ones we dismiss as not being critical. Whether they occur through benign neglect or oversight, every organization needs to take steps to eliminate these potential control breakdowns. In this article we'll take a look at common control failures related to segregation of duties, employee departures and expense reimbursements.

Segregation of Duties

One of the key tenets in a good internal controls program is the appropriate segregation of duties. When it comes to accounts payable, this ensures that no one individual handles or has access to more than one step in the procure-to-pay process. This makes it more difficult for fraud to slip through without some sort of collusion. Two of the most common times when appropriate segregation of duties are overlooked are 1) when an employee is promoted and 2) the exceptions. Let's take a look to see what can go wrong in both these cases.

While we are strong advocates of promoting from within, AP Now cautions everyone that when it is done care should be taken to ensure that the access the employee had in his or her old position is cut off. So, if you have someone who was processing invoices and promote them to handle the master vendor file, cut off their ability to process invoices right before you give them access to make changes to the master vendor file. This one little step is often forgotten in numerous organizations. And, this is not just a mistake made in accounts payable. Organizations make it across the board in all departments.

The second problem that occurs more frequently than we'd like to admit is when companies make one exception to the segregation of duties assignments. Usually they've done an exceptional job setting up their delegations for segregation of duties and then ruin it by making one big exception, usually for either the accounts payable manager or the controller. Unfortunately, this negates all their good work. They usually have a plausible excuse for this departure, but not one good enough. At the end of the day, the need for appropriate segregation of duties trumps ease of operation and the like.

Departing Employees

Whether the company is dancing the proverbial jig or crying buckets over an employee who is leaving the company, the steps it should take with regard to internal controls are the same. These steps are rarely taken. When someone leaves an organization, you should:

1. Immediately cut off their system access.
2. Get all credit cards back. This includes T&E cards, fuel cards and any corporate procurement cards.
3. Notify the bank immediately and cancel all cards. Remember, just because the employee returned the credit cards, doesn't mean the credit card numbers and expiration dates weren't written down before the cards were turned in.
4. If the departing employee had any signing rights for checks or could approve or initiate wire or ACH transactions, immediately suspend those rights. Call the bank and follow up with a written notification.
5. If you enter your employees in the master vendor file for expense reimbursement purposes don't forget to deactivate them when they leave the company so they can't slip through one last unauthorized expense report.

Expense Reimbursements

The IRS has strict requirements about what's required as documentation of expenditures for accountable plans. So, when it comes to expense reimbursements, it's not only a matter of internal controls, it's also a matter of endangering the organization's accountable plan status. And to be fair, this is also an issue of what the organization feels it should pay for and what the employee should pay for.

The first concern is that of who attended a business event. IRS requires the listing of every attendee at a business event. This information should include not only their name, but their title, name of their organization and business relationship with the organization. Your employees should include this on their expense reimbursement requests. Verifying this is difficult if not impossible, but you can get an idea of how many people attended – if you get the detailed meal receipt. That will show how many main courses were ordered. This is not a perfect control but probably the best you can do. We should also note that not every organization is willing to do this kind of verification although we are seeing a growing number request the detailed meal receipt.

The detailed meal receipt can also be used to verify that no employee has surreptitiously added a gift card when taking a guest out for a meal at the company's expense. One would hope that if the organization required the detailed meal receipt, employees would be smart enough not to include a gift card for themselves.

The last overlooked expense reimbursement issue involves what was really ordered. When an employee submits an expense report with only the total amount showing, there's no way to tell what actually was ordered. Two examples shared by our readers bring home the point. One involves an employee who frequently put in for business entertainment on a Friday night. When the detailed meal receipt for one particular Friday night was obtained it showed two adult meals and two kiddie meals. This makes one wonder who actually was at that dinner. The second involved what was supposed to be a job discussion.

The receipt showed a plate of wings and a dozen beers.

Do all employees play these games? We do not believe so; in fact, we think the number that does is a small minority. However, we have seen an increase in the number of companies requiring the detailed meal receipt and we can only think it is to address issues such as those discussed here. Please remember, that just because you require all receipts or the detailed meal receipts doesn't mean you have to check them all. The purpose of requiring the receipts is to serve as a deterrent to those employees thinking of ordering something they shouldn't. Spot checking of receipts is typically sufficient.

Strong internal controls protect any organization. It is important to make sure yours cover the often over-looked people issues.

When Internal Controls Breakdown: The Process

Even organizations that believe they have tight internal controls, more than occasionally have a breakdown in controls. That's because there are a few areas that are sometimes overlooked when it comes to implementing appropriate segregation of duties and strong internal controls. Let's take a look at five places that happens in the accounts payable process.

Breakdown #1: Master Vendor File Access

The master vendor file if handled properly can serve as a strong fortress in protecting your organization against many types of fraud and duplicate payments. However for this to work, access to it for purposes of updating existing information and adding new vendors must be severely limited.

Unfortunately, in more than a few companies anyone processing an invoice can enter a vendor into the master vendor file. They can also change data on existing vendors. Even if no one tries to play games, unlimited access inevitably means vendors in the file more than once, increased chances of duplicate and/or erroneous payments and the possibility of fraud.

While it is certainly easier to simply let processors enter new vendors as they see fit, it is not a good practice.

Breakdown #2: Not Insisting on Rigid Coding Standards

One of the most common ways an organization pays twice is when its processors all don't process invoices in the same manner. This means entering data the exact same way. In order to ensure this happens in your organization, the development of a rigid coding standard for data entry both when processing invoices and when entering data in the master vendor file is critical. It is the first line of defense.

When the coding standard is developed, it should address every possible situation that might occur in the data. This includes dealing with punctuation, abbreviations, spaces, dashes, middle initials, DBAs, invoice numbers etc.

Once the standards are developed and shared with processors, there should be a periodic check to make sure no one has developed alternate entry standards for their own personal use.

Breakdown #3: Allowing Rush (ASAP) Checks

Every business has emergencies where they must issue a payment immediately. The key is to keep this number to an absolute minimum and employ the same strong controls and processes to the rush item as would be used on an item that goes through the normal invoice processing function. Most importantly this means entering the invoice number for the invoice and extinguishing the associated purchase order and receiving document.

Regrettably many of the rush payment requests are sadly lacking in documentation and backup making it impossible to follow standard invoice handling procedures. If this is the case, documentation should be collected after-the-fact, when it becomes available and the appropriate actions taken.

When the purchase order and receiving document remain open

the likelihood of a duplicate payment (rarely returned by the vendor) skyrockets. For, if an invoice shows up and the processor is able to find an open purchase order and receiving document, they are all set to push the transaction through.

Breakdown #4: Returning Checks to Requisitioners

Returning checks to requisitioners is a nightmare for accounts payable as well as a sign of poor internal controls. In order to return the check, the payment must be separated out of the normal check production cycle. The entire process is inefficient adding time to a process that does not have to be. What's more, a large percentage of checks that are returned to the requisitioner are also Rush checks. So there are two potential places for internal controls to breakdown on these payments.

But the real breakdown in internal controls comes from giving the check to an employee instead of mailing it. Many cases of employee fraud involve an employee insisting on getting the payment returned to them for delivery and then keeping the check and cashing it for personal use.

One of the easiest ways to eliminate a good part of this problem is to insist that all Rush payments be made by electronic (ACH) payment not check. Then there is no check to return. A strong policy of not returning checks works wonders if backed by management. And, finally, if all else fails and there are still requests for checks to be returned, consider developing a form requiring an explanation of why the return is needed. This form should also require an additional signature from a high level executive like the CFO. Ideally, the signature required should be of an individual who supports the "No Return" policy. Just implementing a policy that will require someone to have to go and explain to the CFO does wonders in reducing the number of such requests.

Breakdown #5: Having a Petty Cash Box

Anyone who has ever run a petty cash box probably has at least one hair-raising tale to tell about shenanigans that went on with the box. Inevitably the boxes get out of balance and rarely does that misbalance result in there being more money in the box than there should be. But that's just the beginning of the nightmares associated with petty cash boxes. They are time intensive to operate, the documentation for the reimbursements from the box are often flimsy and verifying the item was reimbursed elsewhere is difficult, if not impossible.

Given the wide use of credit cards and corporate cards, there is really no reason why almost all companies who still have petty cash boxes don't eliminate them. Yet, about one-quarter of all organizations still have them. We've already alluded to the double reimbursement issue, which can be intentional or unintentional. What's more, employees will sometimes put items through the petty cash box for reimbursement that they could not get through on their travel and expense reimbursement reports because of the scrutiny of those reports. If the item can't pass muster on T&E there is no reason for it to be reimbursed through petty cash.

The simple solution to the petty cash box internal control breakdown is to eliminate it. Small expenditures can be repaid through the travel and expense reimbursement process.

If the organization insists on keeping a petty cash box, the amount of cash should be small, the people reimbursed through it should be limited to those who don't ever submit an expense reimbursement request and the amounts limited to a very small amount, say $10 or $25. Lastly, having a petty cash box puts the office where it is located at a slightly elevated risk for theft, if it is widely known the company has cash on its premises.

Concluding Thoughts

Strong internal controls are critical to a well-run accounts payable function. In this section, we've taken a look at some of the ways these controls break down. But these are not the only ways. Hopefully, you'll keep your eyes peeled and constantly evaluate new and existing processes to make sure your organization has the strongest controls possible.

Chapter 11

The New Vocabulary in Use in AP (and Elsewhere in the Business Community)

The evolution in the accounts payable, accounting and business world has brought with it a whole slew of new concepts and terminology to explain those ideas, products, and processes. What follows is a look at some of the new language that has crept into the profession in the last few years. It is loosely broken into the following categories:

- The Accounts Payable Process
- Fraud
- Regulatory
- Technology

The Accounts Payable Process

The first thing you'll notice as you look through the terminology is that some of the items in this category could have possibly been included in other categories. What's important is not which category they are in but that you understand the concepts, so don't focus too much on my somewhat arbitrary groupings.

Dynamic Discounting. Dynamic discounting is an agreement between a buyer and supplier whereby payment for invoices is made early in return for a reduced price or discount. The pact includes the right to vary the discount according to the date of early payment. As you might imagine, earlier payment dates translate into greater discounts. The discounting agreement spells out the relationship between the number of days early and the discount.

Often, but not always, a third party stands between the two providing the financing that makes the early payment possible. The most common form of dynamic discounting is the early payment discount offered by some suppliers; with 2/10 net 30 being frequently offered. But there are many variations depending on industry and other factors. Dynamic discounting, when used effectively, allows all parties to meet their unique needs; there's no one-size fits all approach as there is with traditional early payment discounting.

e-Invoicing. When companies talk about electronic invoicing, it's not always clear what they mean. The term encompasses many different delivery mechanisms. In the strictest sense of the term, e-invoicing refers to the automated process of sending or receiving an electronic document that is the invoice. Sometimes this is referred to as invoice automation.

Today, there are a number of quite attractive third party electronic invoicing options available. Some of these will handle small volumes of invoices as well as large.

Ghost Cards. Okay, this is another term that's been around for a while. That being said, we thought a review of the terminology might be in order for at least a few of our readers. A ghost card is a credit card number that is specific to a company, department, or individual. If the card is given to a company or department, it is for use by anyone in that company or department. For this reason, some refer to ghost cards as cardless accounts.

Use of ghost cards makes it easier to assign the cost of purchased items to specific departments. A ghost card can even be issued to selected suppliers, who charge the card number of every company purchase made through them. Probably the most common example of ghost cards might be for departmental purchase of office suppliers from the local retailer, specializing in office supplies.

These cards are also sometimes referred to as vendor payment cards, virtual cards, or electronic accounts payable.

IFRS. Although not exactly a new term, we thought it might be a good idea to

review some of the changes in the accounting world. Most readers are well aware that GAAP stands for Generally Accepted Accounting Principles. For many years these were the guiding force behind the creation of US financial statements.

The problem arose when trying to compare statements from companies in different countries. It was a nightmare and often they were not comparable.

Thus the tedious process of developing an international standard began. The result is the IFRS, the International Financial Reporting Standards. From time to time you will hear discussion about convergence, referring to the move towards IFRS. Although no timeline has been established for convergence to the standards in the US, the adoption of those standards is starting.

Phantom Duplicates. First, since we believe in giving credit where credit is due, this term and explanation came from Lavante's Joe Flynn. He uses phantom duplicates to describe duplicate vendors in your master vendor file – but not ones that are easily identifiable by standard means.

So, even if you are using rigid coding standards, as prescribed by best practices, these duplicates can sneak into your master vendor file. Typically, they are organizations with very different names. The way you uncover them is by searching for duplicate contact e-mails, duplicate TINs, and perhaps even duplicate contact phone numbers.

When you find the same information on two accounts of vendors with very different names, you know you have a phantom duplicate. This can happen, for example, when a vendor changes names and neglects to inform you or for a variety of other legitimate (and not so legitimate) reasons.

Vendor Self-Service Portal. A vendor portal is an online repository of vendor information. Some reading this may realize that it is a form of a master vendor file. The self-service portion means the vendor inputs its own information itself. Companies that utilize these portals typically collect a lot more information than those that enter the data themselves manually. Updating it is a lot easier. The company that owns the portal simply sends an e-mail dinging all their suppliers asking them to update their data. In an ideal world every supplier would comply immediately. This rarely happens but a larger portion of the data does get updated than in a manual environment.

There has been a move towards self-service vendor portals by best practice companies. Many have built them for themselves to the tune of several million dollars. Recently there has been an introduction of a third-party model bringing this functionality.

Fraud

As you read through this section, you will probably note that many of the terms could have been included in the technology section. They have purposely been set into their own section to emphasize the importance of the fraud issue and the attention it deserves.

Bribery under FCPA. When most people think of bribery they think of the exchange of money for as the medium of exchange. But, this does not have to be, especially when talking about the Foreign Corrupt Practices Act (FCPA), In fact, the Act defines a bribe very broadly as "anything of value." So in addition to money, this might include:

- An offer of employment for the recipient or someone designated by the recipient

- Discounts
- Gifts
- Lavish meals and other entertainment (including trips)
- Stock
- A commission
- Property

What's more, the bribe is still a bribe if it is paid through a third party or is a future payment. These considerations make it all the more difficult for accounts payable to ferret out payments that are really bribes. It is also why it is important to scrutinize expense reimbursements closely.

Corporate Account Takeover. There's been a lot written about corporate account takeovers, but we've never actually defined what is meant by this term. We turn to NACHA, the electronic payments association, for the following definition.

Corporate Account Takeover is a form of corporate identity theft where a business' online credentials are stolen by malware. Criminal entities can then initiate fraudulent banking activity. Corporate Account Takeover involves compromised identity credentials and is not about compromises to the wire system or ACH Network.

A recent survey by the Association of Financial Professionals (AFP) revealed that 14% of professionals responding to the AFP Fraud survey had experienced corporate account takeover last year, with 2% actually suffering a loss.

Cross-Channel Fraud. Essentially, cross-channel fraud involves fraudulent transactions being conducted on multiple channels. This type of fraud is on the rise as fraudsters/fraud crime rings exploit weaker channels.

An example from the accounts payable world is crooks who take positive pay rejects and represent them as ACH debits. In this case the ACH is the weaker channel. Of course, if readers have put ACH blocks on their accounts where appropriate and are monitoring bank accounts daily, this tactic wouldn't work and there would be no weaker channel.

The term is getting a lot of play in the banking community. Expect to see strengthened authentication across the entire banking spectrum.

Hacking Back. Let me start out by pointing out that as attractive as this concept may be, it is in all likelihood illegal. Hacking back is simply an act of retaliation. It is where a company, without damaging the intruder's network, a company that has been the victim of a cyber-theft retrieves its electronic files or takes action to prevent the exploitation of the stolen information. While this seems to be a reasonable approach at first glance, upon examination, there are some very real problems.

Part of the problem lies in the fact that the crooks sometimes use unwitting third party systems to launch their attacks. This is a legal gray area that is likely to become a topic of debate in some circles. Retaliating would result in an innocent party be harmed.

This is just one more example of how technology is changing not only the way we do our jobs but the way issues are addressed.

Keylogging Software. Some of the discussion about ACH fraud revolves around the downloading of keylogging software. This is a program whose main purpose is to monitor and capture keystrokes. In the case of fraud, the crook is focused on capturing user IDs and passwords. This is the same software sometimes used by parents to track their children's Internet activity and by spouses to catch partner's disloyalty.

The remote program secretly monitors opened windows applications and sends the captured keystrokes information at specified e-mail address in stealth mode or using FTP settings. Unfortunately, no special hardware is required to operate it.

Advanced invisible key stroke logger programs can even monitor typed text, clipboard contents, system startup time, voice chat conversations, sent emails, windows captions and various other system and internet activities.

Mass Marketing Fraud. Mass marketing fraud is a term that's been around for some time. It is used to describe frauds that are perpetrated on the masses using mass communication techniques. In the past, this was primarily telemarketing and bulk mail, two relatively low-tech approaches. That has all changed today.

Now, these scams are run by organized crime and are anything but low-tech. Most of them take advantage of electronic communications and attempt to either trick you into giving them personal and/or banking information or scam it out of your computer.

These crooks are increasingly difficult to catch as they often operate across borders and across the ocean. Just identifying them is a problem; catching them and recovering your money is next to impossible. Thus, it is imperative that everyone learn to identify frauds before they occur.

Ratware. If you are attempting to guess what this new terminology means and are focusing on something not so good, you're heading in the right direction. Ratware software typically obtain legitimate e-mail lists through illegal methods and then use them to spam the recipients using a spoofed e-mail address. But this is taking spam one step further. Most of these e-mails are used to attempt to get money they have no right to. In these cases, the crook sends no product.

Not all ratware programs use legitimate lists. Some will run wordlists to create thousands of potential e-mail targets. If you have a last name that is not unusual, you've probably received a mailing from such a list. They literally create hundreds of thousands of potential targets using this approach.

The e-mail blasts to these targeted lists (whether the crook created them or illegally procured them) are most frequently used to either get your banking information or get you to send money for something that will never be delivered.

Spoofed e-Mail Addresses. A spoofed e-Mail address is created using a forged sender address. The purpose is to deceive the recipient into thinking the message is legitimate. What is truly distressing about this tactic is it is relatively easy to do. The Internet is littered with free e-mail spoofing programs and advice on how to use them.

One way to identify a spoofed email simply hover your mouse arrow over the name in the from column. You will be able to see if the email is from a domain that is linked to the sender name. This is not a 100% guarantee. Really good spoofers can change this as well. Know who you are doing business with and always be suspicious.

Spear Phishing. Spear phishing is a more sophisticated form of the old email phishing scams. By now, most people are savvy about the preposterous email scams purporting all sorts of ridiculousness. Crooks have learned if they want to snag intelligent business professionals, they have to create intelligent business emails – and alas, that is what they are doing.

Spear phishing emails are messages that look authentic like they really came from the party they are imitating. They may even have the company's logo – which the crook simply copied from the Internet. As with other email scams the messages will try to get you to click on a link or download attachment. Either of these actions will lead to the download of keylogging software.

Most recently, there has been a surge of spear phishing emails from crooks pretending to be NACHA, FedEx and UPS.

Vishing and Smishing. No, you have not seen two typographical mistakes. As most readers are aware, phishing is the attempt to get information you have no right to. In the case of payment fraud it usually occurs through a malicious e-mail or computer takeover. But crooks are getting smarter and fewer people are falling for their e-mail schemes or perhaps, email spam filters have gotten better at blocking them.

So now we have two new variants:

1) Vishing - Phone-based version of phishing. and

2) Smishing – Vishing combined with text based messaging.

The reason this matters to AP is this is the next generation of approaches being used by crooks to recruit money mules who facilitate their electronic payment frauds.

Regulatory

Even regulatory issues have been impacted by technology, as you will see when you look at some of the definitions. We've included dormancy period, as it refers to unclaimed property, in this list because although it has been around for quite some time, a number of professionals are not familiar with the concept.

ACA. ACA stands for the Affordable Care Act, or more fully the Patient Protection and Affordable Care Act. The odds of it impacting the accounts payable operations are high for those of our readers located in the United States.

The reason for this is simple. There is certain reporting that will be required under this Act and many professionals believe this reporting will either be done by the insurance providers, who will likely charge for this reporting, or the organizations required to report it themselves.

Should the reporting fall on the shoulders of the organizations, for whatever reasons, most experts believe it will end up in the same organization that currently does the 1099 reporting. This is one of the evolving issues that those responsible for the accounts payable function should stay on top of – and of course, AP Now is closely following it for its readers.

Click Through Nexus. Expect to hear a lot about click through as Amazon and other online retailers fight with many of the states over collecting sales tax for online sales. Traditionally nexus was established by a physical presence and a few other business arrangements. But, given the volume of online sales, the battle for sales tax revenue is now focused at online sellers and their affiliates.

Click through nexus means exactly what it sounds like; the establishment of nexus and hence the responsibility to collect and remit sales tax for an online sale. Out of state sellers will be deemed to have established nexus when a resident of the state clicks through and makes a purchase. They will then be required to collect and remit sales tax, if the state in question adopts click through nexus laws.

Creeping Nexus. For a long time, we simply had the concept of nexus. Then, thanks to the explosion of Internet purchases, we had a concept of click-through nexus. Now, we can thank the states continued need for additional revenue for the concept of creeping nexus.

Creeping nexus refers to the practice whereby the states redefine terms so that, often without realizing it, a company unintentionally establishes nexus in a location it traditionally didn't have nexus in.

Some of the things that might trigger this nexus might include paying for an employee's home office, attending trade shows for too many days in one state and of course, affiliate relationships such as the one Amazon has with many small businesses. Of course, there is no uniformity in this issue. Like everything else in the sales and use tax world, it varies from state to state.

Dormancy Period. In the discussions about unclaimed property reporting the term dormancy period is frequently used. It is the period of time, during which the holder of the property does not have to take action on the property. The action referred to is the reporting and remitting of the property to the state. Another way to look at dormancy period is it is the amount of time the organization can hold onto the property before it must report it and turn it over to the state. The turning over to the state is also called remitting to the state.

Readers should be aware that the dormancy periods vary by state and by type of property. When it comes to un-cashed checks, there are different dormancy periods for payroll checks, vendor checks, refunds and travelers checks. Occasionally dormancy periods are referred to as abandonment periods.

Economic Nexus. Most are familiar with the concept of nexus, whereby a firm has a physical presence making it liable to the state for income taxes associated with income produced from its presence in that state.In recent times and the advent of online buying and selling, we've seen the introduction of the concept of click-through nexus. Now, states are taking the concept one step further, in a move some believe to be questionable.

A few states are looking to tax companies for what they call economic nexus. These states believe that if a company is economically present in a state if it derives income from a state's market by making sales to in-state customers or receives income from intangible property, such as from a trademark in use in the state, it has economic nexus. It would then be required to pay income tax on those earnings.

It will be interesting to see if the states pushing for economic nexus are successful.

FCPA. FCPA stands for the Foreign Corrupt Practices Act, which prohibits the bribery of foreign government officials. While this is certainly not a new concept, what is new is the role accounts payable is playing in this arena. In growing numbers, companies doing business internationally are expecting/requiring all employees to be cognizant of the law and its impact on their payments. This includes AP.

While virtually no employee in accounts payable is likely to be in a position to offer a bribe to a foreign government official, accounts payable is the last set of eyes to view a payment before a potential bribe goes out the door. For this reason, companies are now starting to require FCPA training for their accounts payable staff as well as those directly involved in business activities.

Technology

This is the longest section in this chapter. As I look over the list of items to be included it brings to mind the fact that more and more the accounts payable function is an integral part of the finance and accounting chain, and not an island unto itself. Gone are the days when the accounts payable department, if very lucky, got the cast-off computers of another department, when the original owners were upgrading. The technology terminology span a wide variety of issues all touching the accounting and accounts payable functions.

Big Data. IBM states that 90% of the data in the world today has been created in the last two years alone. Trying to get your head around that is mind boggling enough. Big data is actually what it sounds like. IT is sets of data so large and complex that they become difficult to work with using existing database management tools. IBM also defines big data by three different variables:

- volume,
- velocity and
- Variety

These are the three Vs of Big Data. Volume, as you might expect, refers to the sheer amount of information, velocity refers to the time sensitive nature of the data and variety, the different types.

Now, if you are wondering about the time sensitive nature of data in AP consider this. In fraud matters, getting the best information as quickly as possible is critical. Expect to hear more about Big Data in Accounts Payable for the foreseeable future. What's more, you'll be hearing a lot about this interesting concept in all lines of accounting and finance as well as some places you might not expect.

BYOC. BYOC stands either for Bring Your Own Cloud or Build Your Own Cloud. Under this approach, corporate employees can utilize their own personal clouds or a combination of public or private cloud services from third-party cloud providers instead of the company's own cloud services.

While BYOC provides employees with the flexibility to store and access data such as documents, images, videos and other files via a wide variety of cloud options, there are some problems, some of which you may have already identified.

The big issues are control and the potential risks to the enterprise when security policies and best practices aren't implemented or followed. This is an emerging practice that we'll follow to see how it evolves and affects the accounts payable function.

Note: Some may also use this acronym for Bring Your Own Computer or in the academic arena, Build Your Own Curriculum.

BYOD. The first time I saw BYOD in a business article, I did a double take. Then I read on and realized I had been mistaken. As you probably are aware, many professionals are buying Smartphones and tablets for personal use. The term "devices" seems to be evolving to cover both of these items. Many buying these devices are bringing them to work to help with their day-to-day work processes. Hence, the evolution of the term BYOD or "bring your own device."

Readers should note that there has been a good deal of controversy over this practice. The concern revolves around the use of these devices to assist in banking transactions and the potential lack of security protocols on the devices. The concern is that use of a device without the proper anti-virus/fraud software might make it easier for a crook to enact a takeover of the company's bank account.

Cloud Computing. Along with everything else that is changing, the language spoken in accounts payable today is undergoing a transformation. You may have heard of a concept called cloud computing. It's not as complicated as it seems. Cloud computing is an Internet-based process where resources are shared and software and/or information is provided to computers on an on-demand basis.

Taking the concept one step further, we are seeing the evolution of "The Cloud" as a central nervous system for a new universal communications infrastructure that is accessed through the Web.

You'll also see references to public clouds and private clouds. This has changed the way many of the applications used in accounts payable are built, purchased and used.

Digital Signature. First, the terms digital signature and electronic signatures should not be used interchangeably. Digital signatures provide much more protection than electronic signatures.

Digital signatures are sometimes referred to as advanced electronic signatures. They take the concept of an electronic signature one step further by marrying it with additional technology that ensures the authenticity of the signer. Some liken the approach to that of an electronic fingerprint.

The beauty of this approach is that it is unique to the signer and the document. If any change is made to the document after the digital signature is put in place, the signature is invalidated.

It is obvious why business likes the concept of digital signatures. It protects the organization against forgeries and tampering with the document.

Dirty Data. While the term has been kicked around for a while in technology circles, it does have serious implications for the accounts payable function. Basically, dirty data is inaccurate, incomplete or flawed data. When it comes to the accounts payable function it can also mean duplicate listings (in the master vendor file), outdated contract information as well as missing W-9s.

If no attempt is made to regularly update contact information what started out as good or clean data will eventually get dirty. This is becoming increasingly an issue as certain new types of fraud become directed at accounts payable.

Dirty data also presents a real problem when issuing 1099s. If the IRS TIN Matching system isn't used to identify mismatches, then B-Notices will abound. Better to clean the data after the mismatch is identified and avoid the problem later on. Expect to hear a lot about dirty data in accounts payable given the explosion of data analytics and the plummeting costs associated with the process.

RBI. Cloud computing has brought whole different way of looking at things. Rosslyn Analytics has pioneered a new concept: Return-Before-Investment (RBI). It is used by companies to calculate not only the total cost of upgrading reporting systems by adopting cloud analytics, but to determine (using a data maturity model) where value will be created by whom within the company and when. It is quite common for organizations to realize significant value within days of subscribing to cloud analytics – well before any payment for the new platform has been made.

In summary, traditional ROI models show what you have to invest before you are even able to assess what value you might get out while RBI measures the benefits of what you get out immediately – before even paying for the first seat/license. We expect to hear a lot more about this intriguing concept.

Straight Through Processing. While many of our readers have heard the term Straight-through-Processing (STP) in different talks by professionals discussing e-invoicing or e-procurement, we thought it worthwhile to discuss exactly what is meant in the invoicing world. The idea behind STP is the elimination of both human intervention and hopefully errors at the same time. In this case the human intervention applies not only to the processor handling the invoice but also the approver.

It cuts out manual processes and increases the speed at which an invoice can be processed, although not necessarily paid. Appropriate payment terms can still be incorporated into the process. In theory an e-invoicing model is married to an e-procurement process and the process will be seamless and error-free. Organizations gain control and visibility over finance and procurement processes and improve overall process performance.

Virtual Desktop Infrastructure. Desktop virtualization is an emerging approach that splits the desktop environment and the associated application software from the physical device that is used to access the applications. The flexible nature of this arrangement allows companies to meet the growing challenge of adequately providing access to applications and information for employees working remotely.

The benefit of this approach comes when employees use their own devices (computers, laptops, tablets or smartphones) and the employee leaves the organization. Companies can remove business applications and data if the employee leaves the organization, without affecting the person's personal information and applications.

Concluding Thoughts

The language in the business community is changing along with many of its processes. Keeping up is critical – otherwise you won't even understand what is being discussed.

Chapter 12
The Accounts Payable Function of Tomorrow

The accounts payable function at virtually every organization looks very different today than it did just a few short years ago. If you don't agree consider for a moment the various tasks impacted by email. Today, every organization receives at least a few invoices that way and many receive a large volume. And that is just the tip of the iceberg. What's more, the accounts payable function of tomorrow, the one that will be commonplace five to ten years from now will look very different. In this chapter we take a look at some of the factors impacting that change and what's already happened. These issues include:

- The Environmental Issues Impacting the Function
- The Expanding Role of Technology
- Growing Management Focus on Regulatory Risk and Controls
- The New Finance Factor: Dynamic Discounting

The Environmental Issues Impacting the Function

It seems that anything that can possibly be touched by technology is a lot different than it was just a few short years ago. We watch TV shows and movies on our computers, take pictures with our phones and there's serious talk about a car that drives itself. (I can't wait for that). So, it's really no surprise that the accounts payable function is undergoing a massive transformation, at organizations of all sizes. Let's take a look at what's been going on in the last few years and where the accounts payable function is headed.

Granular-Level Changes in The Last Few Years

For starters, the accounts payable function is no longer an island unto itself. Rarely does the department function in a silo anymore. Today it operates as an integral part of the finance and accounting chain. In some organizations, mainly those that are not heavily dependent on the procurement function for the core business, the accounts payable function and the purchasing department are run by the same person. The procure-to-pay (P2P) function is cleanly integrated and runs much more efficiently when the two arms work together towards the same goal rather than taking divergent paths.

The accounts payable function, in general, has made great strides in the area of reducing duplicate payments. While technology certainly has played a role in this arena, the professionals who work in accounts payable deserve a lot of the credit. By making some very basic changes (mainly insisting on standardization in processing and data entry) the number of straight duplicate pays has plummeted. This doesn't mean there aren't other types of inaccurate and incorrect payments, but the easy errors have been largely eliminated.

The Regulatory Component

At the same time, there have been increased regulatory pressures. These come in two forms. For starters both the states and the Federal government have been quite vocal and active in requiring better compliance with existing statutes. This means those who haven't been complying at all are now being identified (usually through painful audits) and brought into compliance. It also means that those who have been complying haphazardly and not completely are being called on the carpet, again through the painful audit process.

Then there is the issue of constant changes of existing requirements, the end result being that money is turned over more quickly (i.e. reduction in dormancy periods for unclaimed property) or rate changes (in the case of sales and use taxes).

And finally, there are new issues that are either brand new or were on the books but never enforced. The brand new issues include things like the 1099 reporting now required by some states. Both OFAC screening and FCPA have been on the books for years, but have only recently started to get visibility.

The Fraud Component

Unfortunately, fraudsters have also taken advantage of technology to further their "careers." They are using it in ways never imagined before. They understand how the banking process works. They have an intricate knowledge of computers, the Internet and security issues. And they combine all this to develop unique ways to get their hands on funds that do not belong to them.

While the banking and business community have done a fair job at developing products to combat this growing threat, continual awareness is necessary. What's more, employees often take actions which seem harmless but end up exposing the organization to increased risk from these manipulative and conniving crooks.

Implications of These Changes

For starters, it's fairly apparent that automation and technology have been key drivers in the shift that is going on in the business environment in general and in the accounts payable function in the specific. Plummeting costs have put the technology within the reach of just about every organization. The evolution first of SaaS (software as a service) and then cloud capabilities is making a massive difference in who has access from an affordability standpoint.

It also has changed the way the office can be structured. No longer is it necessary for everyone to be located at the same physical location at the same time – although that does remain the norm in most organizations.

Best practices are shifting, evolving quickly to meet the challenges presented by our changing environment. In extreme cases yesterday's best practices have become worst practices and the reverse. More commonly, new best practices are being developed to handle the multitude of new processes, procedures and experiences.

There's also been the emergence of new products and services to meet the ever-changing landscape of the accounts payable function. This is especially true in the fraud arena, where the community is faced with frauds perpetrated in manners never dreamed of in the past. These are particularly perplexing as the perpetrators are often located in other countries beyond the long reaches of the arm of the law.

A Very Different Future of Accounts Payable

The first change we've seen is the emergence of new terminology related to issues affecting the accounts payable function. Readers of this will note that the New Terminology chapter (see Chapter Two). When we started this feature in the Accounts Payable Now & tomorrow newsletter, we had no idea how long we'd be able to continue it. There doesn't appear to be any end in sight. Much of this new terminology relates to technology, but not all of it. To stay effective as a leader in the accounts payable function (and others functions within the accounting and finance chain) it will be necessary to keep current on this.

One massive change we've seen and expect to continue is the emergence of vendor partners who develop specialty products to enhance the accounts payable functionality. Looking back into the not-so distant past, these products were mainly focused on travel and entertainment reporting and duplicate payment recovery. The first e-invoicing products introduced ten to fifteen years ago were on the pricey side, although to be fair some of the cost issues have gone away.

Today there is a wide array of products available to enhance the accounts payable function. The vendors offering them are quite innovative and understand the dynamics of the market. Readers are advised to study their offerings both online and at conferences and wherever possible attend online demonstrations and webinars offered usually for free by these vendors. It's a great way to learn about the latest innovations in the marketplace.

In the past, new technology innovations were often quite expensive, limiting their target audience to only the very largest companies with pockets deep enough to handle the purchase price. Largely, although not completely, the cost issue has changed. Moving forward we expect cost to be less of an issue for more of the innovative products introduced to the market.

To be honest, in the past, requirements of the accounts payable function were not always given the same attention when ERP systems were being developed. That is all changing and today most of the developers realize the importance of the accounts payable function – after all, it's the organization's money.

They are starting to incorporate some of the functionality offered by the specialty vendors in the biggest ERP offerings. We saw this with duplicate payment checking routines. This has been partially responsible for the reduction in duplicate payments.

As time goes on, expect more of these specialty functions to be offered in ERP systems. But make no mistake about it; this is one area where price will most definitely be a consideration. This functionality will not come cheaply.

That being said, for the foreseeable future, there will definitely be a place in the market for the specialty vendors offering their innovative products that help the accounts payable function run more efficiently and effectively.

There is another issue emerging that is likely to change forever the way organizations look at technology. The BYOD (Bring Your Own Device) movement is taking hold with a greater number of employees buying their own devices (smartphones and tablets) and using them for company work. Policies addressing this issue will have to be developed. A few are starting to do that.

With regards to these devices, some organizations are looking to their employees to purchase their own devices and use them for their professional responsibilities. If this approach takes hold (and there is some evidence that it has), questions about security will become paramount. And of course, there will be the issue of getting company data off personal devices should an employee separate from the organization (either voluntarily or involuntarily). Of course, if the data resides in the cloud it may simply mean cutting off access. This type of issue will be on the forefront for the next few years as companies work through the problems and develop policies.

Concluding Thoughts

The next few years will be an exciting time to work anywhere in the accounting/finance chain. For once, accounts payable will be an integral part of the evolution that is going to occur. This is not time to look for a rest. There is a great deal of change coming and this means continual learning, innovation and a lot of hard work. The end result will be greater responsibilities for a smaller staff as transactional jobs disappear and analytical positions become more the norm. The individual who can look into the future, sort through the change and pick out the innovations that will best benefit the organization and then implement those recommendations will be in high demand.

The Expanding Role of Technology

Without a doubt, the relentless march of technology has changed the face of the accounts payable function forever. In all likelihood, it will continue to have an impact in the near future. AP Now isn't really going out on a limb predicting that the accounts payable department of 2020 will look a lot different than the function does today. In this section, we take a look at 20 different ways, technology has changed and continues to impact the way the accounts payable process is handled. While most of the change has been good, you'll note the last item on our list is a definite negative.

1. E-mail communications. Most don't even think of e-mail as a technology innovation but the reality is that it's only in the last decade or so that e-mail has become a standard tool. It helps to reduce the number of phone calls coming into the department and has generally made the staff more efficient.

2. Invoice automation. Third-party or home-grown invoice automation programs were initially very expensive. Today the price has plummeted bringing the cost within the reach of most mid-size organizations. Moreover, many of these programs are available on a pay-as-you-go basis eliminating the huge up-front investment that was often an obstacle in the past. Invoice automation often marries up-front scanning with workflow.

3. Invoices received by e-mail. PDF files now make it possible for organizations from as small as one-person companies up to the very largest to be able to e-mail their invoices to vendors. And that is exactly what is going on. In fact, some companies are refusing to put invoices in the mail claiming it is too expensive. And, they are correct. We expect the e-mail receipt of invoices to become increasingly commonplace and organizations need to adjust their processes to make sure they are ready for this change.

4. Expense reimbursement automation. Like invoice automation, the automation of expense reporting has come down in price drastically. The best of these models check for policy compliance and flag violations. They enable 100% verification without allocating headcount to this tedious task.

5. Internet self-booking of travel. No longer do most organizations book travel through a corporate travel office or a travel agent. In many organizations, employees search for the lowest fares themselves. What's more, online travel services are now offered to the corporate travel market by the companies that handle online booking. Their services are cost-effective, while offering many of the benefits of the traditional travel office.

6. Online verification of mileage. Sites such as Mapquest and other online travel planners provide the staff handling expense reports the ability to verify mileage put in by employees using their personal vehicle for company business. This functionality is being built into the some of the best next generation of expense reimbursement automation products.

7. Online language translators. These online services, usually free, help with the verification process of receipts in different languages. More than one processor has been able to weed out an expense that was clearly personal in nature from a reimbursement request.

8. Scanned receipts. Even organizations that have not dipped their toes into the paperless waters when it comes to invoicing are moving forward having employees scan their receipts for their expense reports. They do this either using a scanner or their cell phone to take pictures of the receipt. The picture is then e-mailed either to the processor or to themselves for attachment to their expense report. Currently, most of the receipts from cell phone pictures are not of great quality, but that is expected to change over time.

9. Remittance advice delivered by e-mail. One of the biggest obstacles in getting vendors to accept electronic payments is the remittance advice needed by the professional handling cash application. Smart companies have set up processes whereby this information is e-mailed and thus eliminated the final step in getting the supplier to accept electronic payments.

10. Self-service portals for vendor information. By having vendors input their own data into your master vendor file, companies solve many problems. It is also easier to get contact information updated and eliminates some of the risk associated with certain types of ACH fraud. Until recently, the only companies who had such portals were the giants who built these vehicles. The cost of these projects was not unsubstantial. However, today, there are third-party models available for a fraction of the cost of developing a home-grown model.

11. Self-service portals for payment status/visibility. The ability to let the vendor check on the payment status of an invoice without calling the accounts payable department is a real plus. This capability is now available sometimes as part of the vendor portal discussed above and sometimes as part of the invoice automation model. Used correctly, it greatly reduces the number of phone calls into the accounts payable department.

12. ACH payments for invoices. Most organizations have long offered their employees the ability to have their paychecks directly deposited into their bank accounts. This same functionality can be used to pay vendors. Handled in accounts payable, not payroll, this practice eliminates a lot of the hassles associated with paper checks. It also gets rid of a lot of paper and it's a less expensive payment mechanism.

13. ACH reimbursement of expenses. While direct deposit of payroll cannot be mandated legally in most states, the same is not true for the reimbursement of travel expenses. Savvy companies do just that eliminating some of the headaches associated with using checks to reimburse employees for out-of-pocket travel expenditures.

14. IRS TIN Matching. Possibly one of the best things the IRS has ever done for business was to make available the use of the program it uses itself to verify name/TIN matches. Companies that take advantage of this free service drastically reduce, if not completely eliminate, the number of B-Notices they receive each year. This makes the accounts payable function more efficient as staff does not have to be allocated to work the B-Notices.

15. Sales and use tax payments to the states via ACH debits. While many probably do not see this as a benefit—and we can't disagree—some of the states have taken advantage of technology utilizing ACH debits to collect the sales and use tax they are owed. Still, it is one more way technology is impacting the accounts payable function.

16. Online unclaimed property listing. Just about all the states now offer online listings of the unclaimed property they are holding. Some only have recent "acquisitions" online and are working on getting back information uploaded. This allows companies to identify and claim their own property rather easily. However, any organization is cautioned against claiming their own unclaimed property if they are not currently reporting and remitting. Putting in a claim will set off a red flag and the ensuing audit will not be pretty. Better to get

your unclaimed property house in order and then put in your claim.

17. Social media in accounts payable. Most of us think of Facebook and LinkedIn as having little business value, although they may help the individual personally. Using social media to find rightful owners of unclaimed property is a lot easier than doing the due diligence required by the states. This works especially well with former employees who might not have received their last pay check or expense reimbursement. This happens frequently when an employee moves at the same time they separate from the organization.

18. Use of personal devices in accounts payable. By personal devices we mean smartphones and tablets. In growing numbers employees have been acquiring these devices themselves and then using them for company business. While on the face of it, this might seem like a generous move on the part of the employee, it could backfire. This is especially true in those instances where strong anti-virus software has not been put on the device. Each company should develop a policy on how they want this issue to be handled.

19. Job listings on LinkedIn. It was just ten years ago that LinkedIn launched the service that most people today use as the basis for their professional networking. What's more, it's the best place for companies to list their open positions and the site most go to when looking for a position. The whole concept of an online professional profile (i.e. resume) was unheard of just a few short years ago. This has changed the way we look for future employees, giving companies the opportunity to check someone out without spending a dime or calling to verify references.

20. ACH fraud via account takeovers. Unfortunately, not all the changes related to technology have been good. Without technology, we would not be dealing with the latest treacherous fraud, which comes into our offices uninvited through our computers. What this means, aside from requiring that everyone be knowledgeable not only about how it is committed but also how to protect against it, is that everyone has to keep updated about the troubles technology can cause as well as the benefits. It's not a one way street.

Growing Management Focus on Regulatory Risk and Controls

Internal controls may sound boring to some but ignore the issue and you'll have a disaster on your hands. Just ask the 'smartest guys in the room' from Enron, Worldcom and Tyco. And before we had that series of debacles we had the derivative blowups that led to the bankruptcy filing of Orange County and others. Yet despite these high profile failures and a basketful of smaller less-publicized ones, getting management to focus on risk and controls has always been an uphill battle – until now.

In its Executive Perspectives on Top Risks for 2014, Protiviti working with the University of North Carolina State University's ERM Initiative, identified regulatory changes and heightened regulatory scrutiny as being the area of highest concern for its survey participants. "Overwhelmingly," says the survey, "respondents signaled their greatest risk challenge surrounds uncertainties regarding regulatory change and heightened regulatory scrutiny. That risk was rated at or near the top no matter how we analyzed the data."

The report goes on to say that "even organizations in industries in which regulations are not typically viewed as having a significant effect, including not-for-profits and governments, rated this risk near the top."

Which Regulatory Issues Impact AP

No two accounts payable departments operate in exactly the same manner. In fact, when it comes to regulatory issues, organizations will divide the work in a myriad of ways. So, when you look at the list below, we may have items included that you do not do. For the purpose of completeness, we're including items that are generally handled in accounts payable. The issues impacting accounts payable can be broken into two groups:

- the ones that have been on the books for a number of years and
- the new ones.

Unfortunately, the second group is continuing to grow!

Older Issues include:

- 1099 reporting
- 1042 reporting
- Unclaimed Property
- Sales and Use Tax
- Sarbanes-Oxley compliance
- OFAC compliance (OSFI in Canada)
- FCPA compliance (anti-bribery legislation in the UK)

Readers should be aware that AP Now has had a number of reports indicating that the IRS is less forgiving than it had been in the past. It expects organizations to know what the law is then conform to it – and that includes reporting regulations.

Newer issues include

- Sunshine Act Reporting
- Conflict Minerals Reporting
- Affordable Care Act reporting.

US readers should be aware that there are a growing number of state reporting issues. This is especially true when it comes to 1099 reporting. A number of the states have their own requisites that do not match Federal reporting requirements.

Additionally, we expect additional industry specific reporting requirements (similar to the Sunshine Act) over time. As you become aware of them, it is critical that you learn everything about them and what will be required of your organization.

Impact on Account Payable

Without a doubt, it means more work. That is obvious. Whether management is willing to allocate additional resources (additional staff and/or additional funding for technical assistance) to regulatory compliance is another issue. However, as most accounts payable departments continue to find ways to streamline their operations through the use of technology, fewer people are needed for transactional processing. With a little training, some of these folks could take over some of the regulatory reporting requirements.

It is critical that they get training and are not just thrown into the reporting quagmire. Clearly, it is important they are taught how to do the task correctly. But, that is only half the reason training is important. It is very likely, given the increased requirements and the greater concern as evidenced by the Protiviti study, that there will be greater prominence given to the accounts payable function, and more specifically the regulatory reporting issue.

Thus, it is critical that this increased responsibility not hurt the reputation of the accounts payable department. This would happen if there were glaring errors made which resulted in fines, penalties and increased regulatory scrutiny on the organization.

Preparation

You can begin by identifying the issues your department is likely to be required to handle. Do not assume that if you have a tax department, they will handle anything tax related. In most cases, this will not be the case. However, sometimes issues will be handled elsewhere. For example, in a few companies, 1099 reporting is handled in payroll not accounts payable.

The section below contains a seven-step action plan any organization can use to make sure it stays on top of the growing number of regulatory issues facing it. These issues will put accounts payable in the spotlight. Make sure you use that prominence to forward the goals of the department and not set it back into the dark ages.

A Regulatory Compliance Action Plan

- Step 1: Identify the issues.
- Step 2: Identify subject matter expert on your staff.
- Step 3: If possible, identify a backup person or two.
- Step 4: Find training on the issue.
- Step 5: Send staff to the training (including the backup person)
- Step 6: Keep up-to-date on regulatory issues being handled in AP.
- Step 7: Identify new compliance issues as they arise.

These issues will put accounts payable in the spotlight. Make sure you use that prominence to forward the goals of the department and not set it back into the dark ages.

The New Finance Factor: Dynamic Discounting

The age old payment timing conundrum has intensified. Suppliers want their money faster than ever while their customers are doing everything they can to hold onto their money longer. With an increasing number of management teams looking to extend payment terms, this is an issue set to explode. Vendors are becoming increasingly vocal about their displeasure with vendors who unilaterally announce they have extended terms and suppliers can take it or they will take their business elsewhere. Dynamic discounting is a methodology to satisfy both parties, even though they have seemingly divergent goals. It is just one more type of supply chain financing.

Background: Early Payment Discounts

Early payment discounts have been around for a long time.

They are coveted by most accounts payable groups as they represent a very attractive rate of return in exchange for an early payment on an invoice. However, they are offered at the discretion of the seller and there is usually little the customer can do to get a vendor who doesn't offer early pay discounts to offer them.

That's because as good a rate of return as the early pay discount is for the purchaser, it is an equally poor rate for the seller. As most readers are aware, 2/10 net 30 is equivalent to a 36% rate of return in exchange for paying 20 days early. This is definitely a zero sum game and across the board sellers seem reluctant to start programs, if they do not already have one in place.

This is not to say they don't want to be paid early. They most definitely do. They just don't want to pay 36% to get it.

The Flip Approach

Dynamic discounting takes the age-old practice of offering early pay discounts and turns it upside down. In this scenario, it is the buyer who offers the seller the option to get paid early – at a discount. At least in the current interest rate environment, the discounts are nowhere near as large as those traditionally offered with early payment discounts.

Dynamic discounting is an agreement between a buyer and seller. In exchange for a price reduction, the purchaser agrees to pay earlier than the normal payment terms. The size of the discount depends upon how early the payment is made.

The Basic Requirement

For dynamic discounting to work effectively for your vendors, invoices must be processed and approved promptly. For without quick turnaround on invoices, a dynamic invoicing program loses much of its value.

Thus you will often see dynamic discounting offered in conjunction with an e-invoicing program. In fact, some of the third party e-invoicing service providers are integrating a dynamic invoicing feature in their product. This is not to say the e-invoicing service provider is offering to fund the discounting program. That needs to be worked out.

How It Works

The vendor decides whether or not to take advantage of the dynamic discounts offered. The vendor makes the call, invoice by invoice. So, they can use it when they want and decline at other times. Some will use it seasonally to smooth out their cash flow and others will use it depending on the rate offered. Still others may choose to never use it.

Once the suppler decides to take the early payment on a particular invoice, they will be paid (usually electronically) the discounted amount. Typically, this is done online using a portal approach. In fact, sometimes when you hear the term vendor portal, it will mean an invoice processing portal that includes dynamic discounting, although that is not always the case.

Inevitable the question of who provides the funding comes up. There is no simple answer. Sometimes the customer self-funds, other times there is a bank involved and more recently, some of the e-invoicing service providers, such as Basware include dynamic discounting as part of their service.

When it is not self-funded, the rate will depend on the credit worthiness of the buyer rather than the seller. This can be a real advantage in those situations where the purchaser's credit rating is significantly better than that of the seller.

Why Consider Discounting

The seller gets their cash faster thus improving their cash flow. Consequently, there is less risk of nonpayment and fewer resources spent monitoring those receivables.

For the credit, collections and receivables staff at the vendor, DSO is reduced. For some this will be an extremely important consideration. That is because for some credit folks, their bonus is calculated on how well they manage DSO. So, in these cases, there might be a real incentive to take advantage of discounting programs.

There can be some real advantages for the buyer, as well. Typically the effective rate of return is better than they would receive on other investments. This will appeal to the finance folks.

But there are benefits for the accounts payable and procure-to-pay staff as well. For starters, the requirement that invoices be approved in a timely manner takes some of the contentiousness out of their relations with other departments. The pressure to approve will come from other sources such as the suppliers themselves, management and finance.

They will have to spend less time responding to vendor inquiries, especially those where's-my-money calls. For most dynamic discounting programs include a payment status portal where vendors can see when their invoices are scheduled to be paid before deciding whether or not to take advantage of the dynamic discounting offered.

Concluding Thoughts

As you can see, there can be some real benefits to both parties when taking advantage of a dynamic discounting program. While this may not be a perfect match for every organization there are definitely pockets of applicability where it would provide a very welcome alternative. Whether it is right for your organization will take a bit of analysis and investigation to make sure you have all the pieces in place.

Chapter 13
The Future of the Professionals Working in and Managing the Accounts Payable Function

Clearly, an important component in any accounts payable depart is the staff of professionals who not only handle the day-to-day responsibilities but also those who manage the function. With the business world changing and evolving, it is critical that professionals who want to stay relevant and employed need to do the same. In this chapter, we take a look at the department of tomorrow and the type of person who will be in demand to work in the accounts payable department of the future. Finally, we'll look at the what's needed to prepare for the future.

- Who Will Be In Demand
- Taking a Customer-Service Approach in Accounts Payable Pays Off
- Career Advancement Advice
- Are You Prepared to Lead the AP Function of Tomorrow?

Tomorrow's AP Department

Without a doubt, technology will continue to make inroads into the accounts payable department. The result of this will be a smaller number of transactional jobs. While some of the people who handled transactional work in the past will make the transition to the new environment, the likelihood is high that the average accounts payable department will be smaller with fewer people doing more varied work.

At the same time technology is decreasing the number of people needed to handle transactions, regulatory issues are ramping up. This is due to the fact that both the states and Feds are becoming increasingly focused on getting every organization to pay its fair share and comply with existing regulations as well as new regulations that must be complied with. There is specific knowledge needed to handle these tasks and the regulations change frequently, requiring constant updating.

Companies in growing numbers will recruit people who they believe can take action and make changes needed. Increasingly, there is a requirement for a BA or BS to work in AP and in some instances companies asking for MBA for managerial positions.

Who Will Be in Demand

The demand will be for well-rounded individuals who do not operate in a silo but understand the impact accounts payable policies can have on other departments within the organization. The professionals who are in the most demand are those who can create solutions to problems and can implement them as well. Having said that, sometimes education is the factor that holds people back as a growing number of organizations are demanding college degrees and a few insist on MBAs for managerial positions. We're also seeing the emergence of certificate programs, which do not have a CPE requirement for maintenance.

Those who can demonstrate achievements and savings for their company and are results driven will find their career paths run smoother especially if they create profiles and/or resumes that speak the language of management: money. The ability to identify problems, create solutions and implement those solutions in a cost-saving manner will be critical to success.

What's more, visibility and lack of transparency are key issues every professional needs to be aware of. Be careful not to shoot yourself in the foot. Be aware of what you put online; it can be seen by anyone at any time.

Staying Current: A Necessity

More than ever before, keeping current with all the issues related to accounts payable is more important than ever. This is not limited to best practices affecting the function but also fraud, regulatory issues, and technology.

Fraud has taken on a particularly onerous note as new frauds relying on technology continue to emerge just as quickly as the business and financial community develop protections against the last new fraud. This means accounts payable professionals not only have to be cognizant of the most recent frauds but also of new practices and products that combat these ugly crimes.

The advances in technology are impacting the accounts payable function by leaps and bounds. Keeping up with these changes is no easy feat. Vendor webinars are often free and provide busy professionals with an excellent opportunity to see how the products work, without having to leave their offices. Many have an educational component, as well.

Preparing for the Future

The desirable positions in accounts payable in the future will require a greater level of understanding and expertise, not only of accounts payable but also related areas. These include accounting, information reporting, unclaimed property, sales and use tax, general ledger and purchasing—to name a few. This is on top of staying current on the changes in technology affecting the function and new frauds and the steps you need to protect the organization against these new threats.

Clearly, what this means is that lifetime learning is a philosophy every upwardly mobile professional needs to incorporate into their professional identity. There's a wider spectrum of skills that will be required, and keeping up in all of them will take some doing. But, it is not an impossible task.

It's probably not a bad idea to keep a list of all the classes, webinars, seminar and conferences you attend as they can be used to demonstrate you've kept current. With conferences, you might even note which sessions you attended. We're not suggesting that you list all this stuff on a resume, but rather use it to gauge when you might need to get additional training in a particular topic.

To help with these issues don't overlook certification and certificate programs. While certification typically requires a certain number of continuing professional education credits (CPEs) each year, certificate programs usually don't. There are pros and cons to each approach. While the necessity of accumulating CPEs might seem like a royal pain, it kind of forces you to stay current in the process.

Your knowledge base is not the only aspect of your career that needs regular attention. There is also visibility issue as well. Every professional, whether they are looking for a new job or not, is advised to have a LinkedIn profile and to connect with others in the field using it. LinkedIn makes networking much easier, especially for those who are reluctant to take an aggressive stance in this regard. By regularly participating in the discussion forums, you can gain some visibility for your thoughts and meet other professionals as well.

When you return from a conference, don't overlook the golden opportunity to link to others you met and might want to stay connected to. Send them an invite mentioning your meeting and see if they are willing to link to you. Almost without exception, you'll find your invitations accepted.

As by the above discussion, networking will become more important than ever. Already most experts believe that over half the available jobs are never listed and are filled simply by word of mouth. Another huge chunk is listed on LinkedIn. Do not overlook the networking benefits of volunteering. This can be with a professional association or at a charitable group that needs help. You may be quite surprised to find out whose volunteering right next to you.

The future for professionals involved in the accounts payable function is changing. Most of the evolution can be positive – if you take the right steps.

The Future of Accounts Payable: Are You Prepared?

Getting ready for the future of the accounts payable demands a huge shift not only in attitude but in skills. It's not that those working in the function do not have the ability to make the shift; most do. The question is: are they taking the necessary steps to make the strategic shift required to evolve into a successful player in the new accounts payable world. A little further on we have a quiz designed to help readers identify those areas that will be important in the coming years as well as figure out where they might need to beef up their skills—or acquire new ones.

Before we get to the quiz, we thought it would be a good idea to take a look at where the function is heading and what types of professionals will be in the most demand.

Where is Accounts Payable Heading?

Without a doubt, technology and automation are making a huge difference in the way the accounts payable function is being handled. At a high level consider the following (which are becoming more common place every day):

- E-invoicing – invoices being accepted electronically using proprietary and third-party models, as well as invoices e-mailed as PDF files.
- Payments - made with ACH to vendors in growing numbers as companies look to get away from paper checks.
- Vendor portals – to handle information stored in traditional master vendor files. These are now of the self-service variety and are often created by third-party vendors.

- Crooks using technology- with an intricate understanding of the banking system taking advantage of nuances and viruses to get their hands on funds that do not belong to them.

There is a steep learning curve associated with some of the technology. Although it is relatively easy to use and adapt to, it is changing quickly as is the adaptations for the accounts payable function.

At the same time, technology is helping regulators do a better job at finding those not complying with all the state and federal requirements. The increased regulatory pressures have shown no signs of abating and what's more, it seems as though additional issues are being added on a regular basis.

While accounts payable was always part of the accounting function, it in increasingly becoming a more integral part of the finance/accounting chain. This is a good long-term development for those who work in the function but it also requires a greater understanding of the related accounting issues.

Impact on the Future

The implications for the future are obvious. Without a doubt, there will be fewer transactional positions, even at smaller organizations. While technology has always impacted large companies, the costs have dropped drastically and everyone is affected. No longer are the changes just for the big guys; they are for everyone.

This means that the nature of the work in accounts payable will shift. While there will still be some data entry type work, expect it to diminish with each passing year. The focus will turn to dispute resolution, which will finally receive the attention it deserves. What's more, there will be an increased managerial concentration on implementing new and effective processes.

However, there will be more analytical work, requiring a slight increase in the number of accounts payable analysts. The people who snag those positions will have to have a broad based understanding of all areas affecting and affected by accounts payable. And, they will need a very good understanding of the latest technology.

Taking a Customer-Service Approach in Accounts Payable Pays Off

As much as I hate to admit this, more than a few accounts payable departments have a less-than-stellar reputation within their organization and with their vendors. This can be partially attributable to the way they interact with their "customers." Now, if you are thinking, "now wait just a minute, we're the customer," you are technically correct. In the transaction itself your organization is most definitely the customer. But we're taking a bigger picture view in this matter. In this section we'll take a look at who we think accounts payable's customers are, what we mean by a customer-service approach and why it is so important to treat them correctly.

Who are AP's "Customers"?

Now, before you say that your organization is the customer and why are we even talking about this, realize that we are looking at this on a granular level. Generally speaking, accounts payable has three broad sets of customers. They are:

- Vendors calling looking for information about invoices
- Employees calling looking for information about their expense reports
- Employees calling looking for information about vendor payments

They can be viewed as customers because accounts payable provides them with a service, usually in the form of information. By treating them respectfully and getting them their information quickly, everyone benefits. This is discussed in detail below.

Don't Become a Doormat

While we emphasize getting the customer information quickly and politely, this does not mean doing whatever is asked. What it does mean however, is that information (whether it's good or bad) is provided in a timely manner. This is done within the guidelines of running an efficient accounts payable operation that incorporates strong internal controls.

Remember, at the end of the day, the accounts payable group is charged with guarding the organization's assets. So, if a vendor calls and asks (or demands) to be paid early, firmly and politely tell them no. If an employee comes running in at the last minute requesting a rush payment for a tardy expense report, the answer is also a polite no.

To address these issues it is imperative that both employees and vendors know what your requirements are. If they are educated to the cut-off schedule for check requests, the payment terms and other information affecting the payment process, these unpleasant situations are less apt to arise.

Benefits of a Customer-Service Approach

The advantages of taking this approach to dealing with those who interact with the accounts payable staff are numerous. Let's take a look at some of them.

- Improves vendor relations. For starters, if people come to expect an efficient response from the accounts payable staff, relations with vendors will get better. This won't happen overnight, but it will occur over time.

- Resolve discrepancies faster. Once relations with vendors improve, it will become easier to resolve discrepancies. If vendors don't dread talking to your staff, they will respond more quickly and will be more likely to try and resolve issues in an equitable manner, rather than taking a high-handed approach. Also, they won't be dragging along any baggage from prior encounters. As with the improvement in vendor relations, this won't happen overnight.

- Earn more early pay discounts. If you are able to resolve discrepancies quickly, you will earn more early payment discounts. Also, as your relationships with other employees in the organization improves, they too are likely to respond faster to your inquiries making it easier to earn those coveted early payment discount.

- Get fewer late fees assessed against your account. If discrepant invoices are resolved before the payment date and payment is made on time, there will be no need to assess late fees. Even though many companies don't pay late fees, many suppliers do asses them and use unclaimed vendor credits to wash them away.

- Receive fewer second invoices. Time spent handling and identifying second invoices and making sure they are not paid is time that could be spent on more value-add functions. If discrepancies are resolved quickly and invoices paid on time, the vendor won't send that dreaded second invoice.

- When operations run smoothly, there are fewer vendor complaints to deal with. That's a win-win for both customer and supplier.

- When problems are resolved quickly, there's less resources needed for that function leading to a more efficient accounts payable function. This translates directly into an improved bottom line for the organization as it spends less on resolving problems related to accounts payable. And, improved profitability benefits everyone.

- Occasionally, even the best run operations run into problems. Sometimes, in order to get those issues resolved, help is needed from the vendor. If you have a good relationship with the vendor they are going to be more apt to help and to pitch in quickly when you have a problem.

- And lastly, the reputation of some accounts payable departments leaves a lot to be desired. Whether it's the staffs fault or not is beside the point. By taking a customer service approach towards both internal and external customers, the image and stature of accounts payable department and staff will improve. Rome wasn't built in a day and repairing a tarnished reputation won't happen overnight either. However, by slowly plugging away at the issue, the department will start to be viewed in a much better light. This is just a side benefit, but a nice one.

Career Advancement Advice

What we've got here are ten tips that are all about you and your career. Incorporate as many as you can and watch your career skyrocket. We've got the resolutions listed first followed by a brief explanation of why each of these resolutions makes good career sense.

The Resolutions

1. Take greater care when writing emails – both in checking spelling and grammar and not responding quickly to an infuriating message.
2. Give at least one talk this year, if you have never given one before; give three or four if you have.
3. Improve your PowerPoint skills and include PowerPoint presentations not only when you are giving a talk but also when making a presentation to management.
4. Make better use of pivot tables when analyzing data and making management presentations.
5. Increase networking using Linkedin.
6. Join at least two groups on LinkedIn and contribute to those forums asking and/or answering queries posted by other participants.
7. Attend at least three vendor webinars during the year.
8. When attending an industry or vendor meeting, don't stay with the folks you know from your current company.

9. Read one book per quarter to help increase your knowledge and advance your career.
10. Take a long hard look at your work wardrobe and honestly evaluate whether it says "I'm management material" or not.

The Importance of Each

Let's take a look at the reason why each of these was included along with the potential benefits of each.

1) You'd be surprised how many spelling and grammatical mistakes are made in emails simply because the person was in a hurry. Unfortunately, it is difficult to see your own errors but other people's jump out at you. That is exactly what will happen when your email with a typo ends up in the hands of one of your senior executives. It will leap from the page making a bad impression. Along the same lines, take five minutes (or better yet, 15) before responding to an email that leaves you seething. Often we will say something in anger that would never be said if we'd had a chance to calm down. Give yourself that time to calm down.

2) There's no better way to build your platform than to give a talk in a professional setting. Now before you start thinking, "I could never do that," realize you can start small. This might mean giving a talk to your department or perhaps a local group you belong to outside work. If you are either really terrified or just want to practice, consider Toastmasters.

3) Beef up your presentations to management by including a PowerPoint presentation. A well prepared PowerPoint can supplement your presentation and bring your point home in an authoritative manner. So, brush up on your PowerPoint and if you don't know how to use it, learn how.

4) Similarly, a well-crafted pivot table can make all the difference while simultaneously showcasing your skills as a professional to be taken seriously.

5) Most people need to network more than they do. It's hard for many to do but LinkedIn has made the process easier. Sign up and post your information, keeping in mind that everyone will be able to see the data you share. Once you've signed up, make sure and periodically update your information – especially if you are doing something new and exciting. You are also ready to link to the folks you know. So, start searching and sending invites. Before long, you'll start receiving invitations to link as well.

6) Once you've joined LinkedIn, don't stop there. Signing up is just the first step. Join a few of the online groups. You may have to explain why you want to join or how you fit in. Most are very easy to join. Once you've joined, participate in the discussions. If someone asks a question that you can answer, jump in and share your expertise. And if you've got a work-related issue, post your question in your group's forum and see what your peers have to say.

7) Not everyone sees the value of vendor webinars. That is unfortunate. They provide a wealth of information and are almost always free. You not only learn how the vendor's product works, you'll get the latest information about the related issue. What's more, some vendors offer educational events with only a brief product overview at the end. Possibly the best reason for attending a vendor webinar or online product presentation is you get to see the product without having to spend a long time with the salesperson. Only after you have narrowed your search would you have the salesperson visit.

8) It's much easier to go to an event with someone you know that to attend alone. But, you'll get much more networking value if you don't stick with the folks you work with but venture out to make new contacts. If there is a lunch, find a table with an empty chair and ask the group if you can join. Introduce yourself to others at the table and participate in the conversation. When the discussion appears to be lagging ask a question that the group can debate about. If you plan in advance, you can have a few ice-breaker questions prepared ahead of time.

9) While it's critical that you keep up on the latest developments in your field, that's just the beginning. You also need to advance your career and get the latest career advice. This might mean reading a book specifically designed to provide professional guidance or it might mean reading the biography of a great leader or innovator. Make it a priority to stretch your mind, focusing on issues other than those directly related to your profession.

10) When was the last time you took a cold hard look at the clothes you are wearing to work? Are some of them well past their prime and perhaps shouldn't be gracing the walls of an office except perhaps if you are taking inventory? It's not easy to let go of favorite outfits but that is exactly what you need to do if they do not present you in the best professional light.

Usually when we have lists like this we say you should pick a few items and try and focus on them. This time, we'd like to suggest you pick all the suggestions on the list that you are not currently integrating in your routine – that's right, all of them.

Are You Prepared to Lead or Manage the Account Payable Function of Tomorrow?

At a minimum, employees will be expected to have the latest knowledge in all areas just to hold onto their current position.

This means continued learning. Lifetime learning will be a necessity for those who want to work a full 40 or so years..

Employers will look for professionals who both have good ideas and who can implement those concepts. Professionals who meet all three criteria will be the best situated for long-term permanent employment. It's not a pretty picture, we concede. But it will be a really interesting ride for those who can meet the grade. Are you prepared? Take AP Now's Preparing for the Future Diagnostic to see if you are on track and where you might need a little help. This was previously published in the Do-It-Yourself Accounts Payable Consultant Handbook, which contains numerous diagnostic checklists that can be used to identify problem spots and/or weaknesses in your accounts payable function.

AP Now's Preparing for the Future Best Practice Diagnostic

1) Do you stay on top of the automation issue as it applies to the accounts payable function? _____ Yes _____ No

2) Do you regularly attend free vendor webinars to see what's available and/or learn about the latest innovations offered by vendors in the accounts payable space? _____ Yes _____ No

3) Do you keep updated on the latest information reporting (both 1099 and 1042-S) requirements? _____ Yes _____ No

4) Are you aware of all your sales and use tax reporting and remitting responsibilities and do you keep updated on them? _____ Yes _____ No

5) Do you stay on top of your unclaimed property reporting and remitting requirements? _____ Yes _____ No

6) Do you regularly check for OFAC violations before making payments? _____ Yes _____ No

7) Have you instructed your staff (and kept up to date, yourself) on how to find potential FCPA violations? _____ Yes _____ No

8) Do you regularly read publications that cover accounts payable issues? ____ Yes ____ No

9) Are you a member of a local or national professional association? ____ Yes ____ No

10) Do you go to meetings of professional associations, conferences and or seminars to network with your peers, as well as learn? ____ Yes ____ No

11) Do you volunteer to help out or hold a leadership position in any professional organization? ____ Yes ____ No

12) Do you look for opportunities and take them to give professional talks? ____ Yes ____ No

13) Do you write articles for professional publications? ____ Yes ____ No

14) Do you participate in online discussion groups devoted to your professional issues – offering intelligent advice rather than simply asking for information? ____ Yes ____ No

15) Do you earn at least 12 continuing professional education credits each year, whether you need them to maintain certifications or not? ____ Yes ____ No

16) Do you have a good understanding of the way your organization's entire accounting system works – not just the accounts payable related areas? ____ Yes ____ No

17) Do you have a decent understanding of how the purchasing function operates at your organization? ____ Yes ____ No

18) Do you understand the interaction between Treasury and accounts payable at your organization? ____ Yes ____ No

19) Do you know the current best practices related to all regulatory issues (information reporting, unclaimed property, sales and use tax etc.) even if they are not handled in accounts payable at your organization? ____ Yes ____ No

20) Have you earned any certifications related to your profession? ____ Yes ____ No

21) Can you articulate clearly not only what the current issues are facing your department, but also several possible solutions?

_____ Yes _____ No

22) Do you regularly make presentations to management?

_____ Yes _____ No

23) Do you know how to create PowerPoint presentations to accompany presentations both at professional gatherings and to management? _____ Yes _____ No

24) Do you have a college degree (BS or BA)? _____ Yes _____ No

25) Are you on LinkedIn? _____ Yes _____ No

There will be a discussion of the best practice responses below. But before you get to that, total up your responses.

Total Score: Yes _____ No_____

How many yesses did you have? Use the chart below to determine how prepared you really are.

- Score 25: You should be fully prepared for the future
- Score 20-24: You are more prepared for the future than the average professional and should be fine.
- Score 15-19: You might want to review the quiz and identify several items to add to your To-Do list for the near future.
- Score 14 or lower: You could have trouble competing in the long stretch. Review the diagnostic above and identify as many new strategies that you can do and begin implementing immediately.

Discussion of Best Practice Responses to AP Now's Preparing for the Future Diagnostic

The higher number of yeses you had to the quiz on the prior page, the better your chances are for professional success. Of course, you still have to execute well, get along with your boss, work for an organization that is profitable and more. But, to get your foot into the proverbial door and climb that ever-slippery career ladder, a higher number of yeses will help get you to the position you want.

1) Automation and technology are making a huge impact on the way the accounts payable function is being handled – at organizations of all sizes, not just the giants. By staying on top of the automation issue as it applies to the accounts payable function you will ensure that you can at least talk intelligently about the issues. You'll also know about the newest innovations, even if your organization is not using them yet.

2) By regularly attending free vendor webinars you'll learn what's available as well as the latest innovations offered by vendors in the accounts payable space. You'll also be able to make intelligent, well-thought-out recommendations.

3) Expect regulatory issues to remain at the forefront for the next few years, if not longer, By keeping updated on the latest information reporting (both 1099 and 1042-S) requirements, you'll be well positioned to identify changes your organization needs to make to stay compliant.

4) Sales and use tax reporting and remitting responsibilities can be tricky, especially as the rules vary from state to state. Keep updated on them or make sure your organization hires an outside organization to do it for them.

5) Staying on top of your unclaimed property reporting and remitting requirements for all states, not just your own, is another good way to make sure your organization stays compliant.

6) Very few organizations regularly check for OFAC violations before making payments, but that is what you are supposed to do. Can you get your organization compliant on that front?

7) Bribing a foreign government official can have serious consequences. By making sure your staff is instructed on how to find potential FCPA violations, you've prepared them to identify possible troublesome payments before the Department of Justice comes knocking at your door.

8) One of the best ways to stay on top of the latest issues is to

regularly read publications that cover accounts payable issues.

9) Membership in a local or national professional association is another good way to keep updated as well as demonstrating you commitment to the profession.

10) Going to meetings of professional associations, conferences and or seminars to network with your peers and learn is a great way to find out what other savvy professionals are doing to advance their career and the accounts payable function in their organization.

11) The benefits of volunteering to help out or hold a leadership position in any professional organization are numerous. It is a great way for others to get to know you and your abilities.

12) Look for opportunities and take them to give professional talks. While this can be nerve-wracking at first, it is a great way for others to get to know you and respect you as an up-and-coming professional.

13) Similarly, by writing articles for professional publications, you can get yourself in front of other companies, including many you have never heard of.

14) By participating in online discussion groups devoted to your professional issues – offering intelligent advice rather than simply asking for information, you will expand your network of professional contacts. This can come in handy should you need help either with a particular project at work or a job search.

15) Certainly you have one hour a month to devote to your professional development. That's the amount of time it takes to earn 12 continuing professional education credits each year, whether you need them to maintain certifications or not. To put it in perspective, CPAs need 40 hours a year – so 12 is really just the bare minimum.

16) By having a good understanding of the way your organization's entire accounting system works – not just the accounts payable related areas, you will be better able to make recommendations that will not adversely affect other

departments. It will also make it easier for you, if at some time you wish to transfer to another department for a better job opportunity.

17) Similarly by having a decent understanding of how the purchasing function operates at your organization, you'll be able to make recommendations that won't throw a monkey wrench into the purchasing operations. You'll also be able to better understand their problems and issues.

18) Increasingly, as wire transfers and now ACH transactions are sometimes being performed in Treasury, an understanding of the interaction between Treasury and accounts payable at your organization will make those transactions run smoother.

19) Do you know the current best practices related to all regulatory issues (information reporting, unclaimed property, sales and use tax etc.) even if they are not handled in accounts payable at your organization?

20) Earning certifications related to your profession demonstrates to your superiors (and potential employers) that you are committed to your profession. What's more, most require you to earn continuing education credits (CPEs) in order to maintain the certification. Thus, it is an ongoing commitment.

21) Today's managers want employees who can both identify problems and solutions. If you can articulate clearly not only what the current issues are facing your department, but also several possible solutions, you will be an employee in demand.

22) By regularly making presentations to management, they will get to know you and your abilities. This opportunity does not often present itself so you need to be ready to grab it when it does occur. Don't fall into the trap of letting your boss do it for you, because you are fearful of speaking in front of a group of higher level executives.

23) By creating PowerPoint presentations to accompany presentations both at professional gatherings and to

management you demonstrate that you are a professional to be taken seriously.

24) Unfortunately, at many companies, a college degree (BS or BA) is the price of entry into management. In some cases without the degree, you won't even be considered for the position. Is this fair? Absolutely not; but it is the reality we live in. If you don't have a degree you can either bolster your credentials by doing as many of things discussed in this article as possible or go back to school at night. There are a number of programs that will give credit for some of your work experience. It's not easy, but it can be done. [And, if you decide to take this route, don't forget to check and see if your organization offers a tuition reimbursement plan].

25) Today, being on LinkedIn is a professional necessity. It is the way people network and the way potential employers find new employees. Some companies block access to social networking sites, including LinkedIn. That should not stop you. You can set up your account and check it from home or from your smartphone or personal tablet.

Concluding Thoughts

The very foundation of the accounts payable function continues to change and adapt to the changing market and business environment. As you can probably tell, technology plays a big part in the future of accounts payable. I hope this book got you to think about your process and possibly create some innovations that you hadn't thought of before reading this work. For at the end of the day, while the primary mission of this book was to share the latest thinking, its ultimate goal was to get the professionals who work in, lead or manage the accounts payable function to contemplate their processes. That reflection should result in some pretty interesting changes.

It's All about Your Bottom Line

Glossary

1042 – Form 1042, an IRS form used for the reporting of annual withholding tax return for US source income of foreign persons

1099 – Form 1099, an IRS form used for reporting income

ACA – Affordable Care Act

ACFE – Association of Certified Fraud Examiners

ACH – Automated Clearing House; term used to describe an electronic payment in the US

AFP – Association for Financial Professionals

AP – Accounts Payable

ASAP Checks – Rush checks or checks to be issues as soon as possible

B2B – Business to Business

B2C – Business to Consumer

BYOD – Bring Your Own Device

CFO – Chief Financial Officer

CPE – Continuing Professional Education

DSO – Days Sales Outstanding

EDI – Electronic Data Interchange

EIN – Employer Identification Number

ERP – Enterprise Resource Planning, for most organizations this encompasses their accounting and financial tracking and reporting systems

FBI – Federal Bureau of Investigation

FCPA – Foreign Corrupt Practices Act

FDIC - Federal Deposit Insurance Corporation

GAAP – Generally Accepted Accounting Principles

IAPP – International Accounts Payable Professionals (now IFO)

IFO – Institute of Financial Operations (formerly IAPP)

IFRS - International Financial Reporting Standards

IRS – Internal Revenue Service (US)

MBA – Masters in Business Administration

NACHA – National Automated Clearing House Association, commonly known as the Electronic Payments Association

OFAC - Office of Foreign Assets Control, a department of the US Treasury

OSFI - Office of the Superintendent of Financial Institutions, an independent agency of the Government of Canada

P2P – Procure to Pay

RBI – Return before Investment

SDN – Specially designated nationals

S-Ox – Sarbanes Oxley Act

STP – Straight through Processing

T&E – Travel and Entertainment, usually used in conjunction with discussions about employee expense reimbursements

TIN – Taxpayer Identification Number

UPIC – Universal Payment Identification Code

URT – Universal Routing Number

W-9 – Form W-9, An IRS form used to request a Taxpayer Identification Number and Certification

About The Author

Mary S. Schaeffer, a nationally recognized accounts payable expert, is the author of 18 business books, a monthly newsletter and a free bi-weekly e-zine, as well as several CPE courses for CPAs. She runs AP Now, a boutique publishing and consulting firm focused on accounts payable issues.

Before turning to writing and consulting she worked in the corporate world as an Assistant Treasurer for the Equitable Life Assurance Society, a Financial Risk Manager for O&Y and a Corporate Cash Manager for Continental Grain.

A frequent and popular speaker at industry live and online events, she has an MBA in Finance and a BS in Mathematics.

About AP Now

AP Now supplies critical information used by professionals concerned about all accounts-payable-related functions and payment issues. Its free bi-weekly e-zine is read by over ten thousand professionals. Information and training are delivered in a variety of mediums - print, online, and in person.

Products/Services

- Newsletter – Accounts Payable Now & Tomorrow is a monthly quick-read publication focused on an emerging accounts payable issue. Each issue contains regulatory updates, an infographic on the state of an AP function and a page of short tips.

- The AP Now Portal – an online repository of articles tips and over 50 diagnostic checklists. Membership in the portal includes the Accounts Payable Now & Tomorrow newsletter,

- Webinars – AP Now runs a robust program of one-hour fee-based webinars. Each month two or more topics are presented using an online delivery vehicle. Subjects covered include accounts payable process and best practices issues, payment fraud, 1099, sales and use tax, unclaimed property and other issues affecting the accounts payable and payment function. NASBA and IFO CPEs are granted.

- Annual webinar pass – For one flat fee, a pass is available which provides access to all AP Now one-hour webinars. NASBA and IFO CPEs are granted.

- Seminars and workshops (live and online) – AP Now also arranges one-day seminars in a variety of accounts payable related topics, including 1099s. These are offered live and online. Where appropriate, AP Now partners with other organizations to produce these events. NASBA and IFO CPEs are granted.

- Books – AP Now's parent, CRYSTALLUS Inc., publishes books related to the accounts payable function. Some of them include *101 Best Practices for Accounts Payable*, *Fundamentals of Accounts Payable*, *Internal Controls in Accounts Payable*, and the *Do-It-Yourself Accounts Payable* Consultant handbook. These are sold by AP Now, the IFO, amazon.com and a variety of other online booksellers. Customized Training – AP Now customizes any of its programs for onsite training. Call 302 836 0540 or e-mail publisher@ap-now.com to discuss.

- AP Consulting – AP Now works with organizations looking to re-engineer their accounts payable process. AP Now also assists service providers in a number of ways, including product development, speaking, and preparation of white papers.

For additional information, visit www.ap-now.com or call 302 836 0540.

Other Recent Books by Mary S. Schaeffer

- 101 Best Practices for Accounts Payable
- Fundamentals of Accounts Payable
- Internal Controls in Accounts Payable
- Preparing for Year End in Accounts Payable
- The Do-It-Yourself Accounts Payable Consultant handbook

Looking for CPEs? Ask your CPE provider if they carry Mary Schaeffer's self-study courses or Internet-based webcasts.

Index

Made in the USA
San Bernardino, CA
08 February 2018